JOHN SCOTT LIDGETT

From a photograph taken in 1930 by E. W. Tattersall

JOHN SCOTT LIDGETT
1854-1953

JOHN SCOTT LIDGETT

A Symposium

by

ERIC W. BAKER
RUPERT E. DAVIES
W. F. LOFTHOUSE
F. C. PRITCHARD
E. GORDON RUPP
ERIC S. WATERHOUSE

edited by
RUPERT E. DAVIES

WIPF & STOCK · Eugene, Oregon

Wipf and Stock Publishers
199 W 8th Ave, Suite 3
Eugene, OR 97401

John Scott Llidgett
A Symposium
By Davies, Rupert E.
Copyright©1957 Methodist Publishing - Epworth Press
ISBN 13: 978-1-4982-8049-5
Publication date 1/28/2016
Previously published by Epworth Press, 1957

Every effort has been made to trace the current copyright owner
of this publication but without success. If you have any information
or interest in the copyright, please contact the publishers.

CONTENTS

FOREWORD vii

BIOGRAPHICAL SKETCH ix

1 THE METHODIST 1
   by Eric W. Baker, M.A., Ph.D.
   SECRETARY OF THE METHODIST CONFERENCE

2 THE WARDEN OF THE BERMONDSEY SETTLEMENT 37
   by W. F. Lofthouse, M.A., D.D.
   FORMERLY PRINCIPAL OF HANDSWORTH COLLEGE, BIRMINGHAM

3 THE BIBLICAL THEOLOGIAN 79
   by E. Gordon Rupp, M.A., D.D.
   PROFESSOR OF ECCLESIASTICAL HISTORY IN THE UNIVERSITY OF MANCHESTER

4 THE EDUCATIONIST 107
   by F. C. Pritchard, M.A., Ph.D.
   HEADMASTER OF WOODHOUSE GROVE SCHOOL

5 THE PUBLIC SERVANT 157
   by Eric S. Waterhouse, M.A., D.D., D.Litt.
   FORMERLY PRINCIPAL OF RICHMOND COLLEGE, SURREY

6 THE ECUMENICAL STATESMAN . . . 183
   by Rupert E. Davies, M.A., B.D.
   TUTOR IN CHURCH HISTORY AT DIDSBURY COLLEGE, BRISTOL

INDEX OF NAMES 211

FOREWORD

OF the contributors to this volume only two, Dr W. F. Lofthouse and Dr Eric S. Waterhouse, have lived long enough to have worked actively with John Scott Lidgett. The rest of us knew him in various capacities, but mostly as the 'old man' of history and legend. Our tribute to him takes the form, not of a biography, but of a series of studies in the impact which he made on the life of the Church and society. We shall be well satisfied if we persuade our contemporaries, and the Church historians of the future, that he deserves a place, with Randall Davidson, William Temple and others, among the great Churchmen of the first half of the twentieth century.

For help of various kinds our thanks are due to:

The Rt Rev. the Lord Bishop of Chichester (Dr G. K. A. Bell)
Mrs V. A. Child
Mrs Gerald Davey
The Rt Hon. J. Chuter Ede, C.H., M.P.
Miss P. M. Elsom
Mr G. P. Gooch
Mrs G. E. Harrison
Dr G. B. Jeffery, F.R.S.
The family of the late Dr C. W. Kimmins
The Rev. R. P. Marshall
Dr H. F. Mathews
The Rev. J. Edwin Reding
The Rev. J. Bernard Sheldon
The Misses Helen and Ruth Simpson
The Rev. D. Hubert Thomas (Assistant General Secretary of the Free Church Federal Council)
The Chief Education Officer of the London County Council
The Editor of the *Methodist Recorder*
The Principal of the University of London

RUPERT E. DAVIES

JOHN SCOTT LIDGETT, C.H., M.A., Hon. D.D., Hon. LL.D.

A Biographical Sketch

JOHN SCOTT LIDGETT'S paternal grandfather was a London ship-owner with a large concern for missionary enterprise and education. His maternal grandfather, John Scott, was twice President of the Wesleyan Methodist Conference, and first Principal of Westminster College for the training of teachers; he was a friend and adviser of Matthew Arnold, who seems to have excepted him from his general description of Free Churchmen as Philistines. John Jacob Lidgett, John Scott Lidgett's father, was a successful man of business in the City of London, but was prevented by an early death from reaching the high position in public affairs and in the Wesleyan Methodist Church to which his abilities and interests were leading him. His wife, never strong in health, though she lived to be very old, bestowed most of her energies on her home, but she helped to found what became the Women's Work department of the Wesleyan Methodist Missionary Society.

Predisposed by this ancestry and parentage to a career in Wesleyan Methodism, education, and public affairs, John Scott Lidgett was born in Lewisham on 10th August 1854, and grew up in Blackheath under the powerful influence of John Scott. The Methodism of his family was the 'Church Methodism' which claimed its origin in John and Charles Wesley, and eschewed the title of Dissent. John spent many of his holidays in rural Yorkshire, and often sang in the choir of Lastingham Parish Church, near Pickering; here he developed an affection for the Church of England which influenced many of his thoughts and actions in later years.

He was educated first at a preparatory school in Blackheath, and then at Blackheath Proprietary School, at that time a flourishing public school. He specialized in Classics from an early age, with the intention of going to Oxford or Cambridge. But his father's death made it necessary for him, in the eyes of his guardian uncle, to go into business in the City at the age of sixteen. Two years later he left an uncongenial post in a firm of insurance and shipping brokers, and entered University College, London, in January 1873. By 1875 he was an M.A. in Logic and Philosophy.

In 1876 he was accepted as a candidate for the Ministry of the Wesleyan Methodist Church. It was deemed unnecessary, because of his already large erudition, that he should study at a theological college, and he proceeded at once to a succession of pastorates in Tunstall, Southport, Wolverhampton, and Cambridge. These controlled his activities for fifteen years, but plans for other things were moving in his mind, and in 1891 he came to London to found, build, and direct the Bermondsey Settlement. He remained in Farncombe Street, Bermondsey, for fifty-nine years, through vast changes in the social structure of London and through two world wars.

But his spiritual and mental energies could not be compressed within the limits of one London Borough or one pastoral charge, however large and important. During his early days in London he took a growing interest in the wider concerns of the Church of which he was a minister, and from the turn of the century was clearly marked out as a coming national leader. In 1908 he was President of the Wesleyan Methodist Conference, and at the same time became Chairman of the London South District of the Church; he held the latter position for nearly forty years. He took an active part in the negotiations at all stages for the union of the Wesleyan Methodist, Primitive Methodist, and United Methodist Churches, and was the first President of the newly united Methodist Church in 1932. He was concerned in all the conversations and discussions, especially in the twenties and thirties, which aimed at the corporate reunion of the Churches of this country. He was President of the National Council of Evangelical Free Churches in 1906, and Moderator of the Federal Council of Evangelical Free Churches from 1923 to 1925.

His literary activities—books, published addresses, articles in magazines and periodicals—were mostly on theological, educational, and social subjects. He was Editor of the *Methodist Times* from 1907 to 1918, and joint Editor of the *Contemporary Review* from 1911 until his death (although he did little editing for the last twenty years).

His profound interest in the education of the people, and not least of its unprivileged members, led to his being elected to the London School Board in 1897, and carried him into the controversy connected with the Education Act of 1902 as one of the leading spokesmen of the Free Churches. He became an Alderman of the London County Council in 1905 and remained so until 1910; he had a second term of office from 1922 to 1928. Throughout his career on the London County Council his primary interest was in education and the subjects allied to it, and he was Deputy Chairman of the Education Committee from 1917 to 1919. But all the affairs of London constituted his political parish, and he both served on many committees of the Council and represented it on other bodies and to many ministries. He was the leader of the Progressive Party on the LCC from 1918 to 1928.

He was a lifelong lover of his own University, and, as usual, translated his love into action. He became a member of the Convocation of London University in 1875, and was elected by it to the Senate in 1922. He was Deputy Vice-Chancellor from 1929 to 1930, and Vice-Chancellor from 1930 to 1932. In the performance of these manifold duties he must have come as near to ubiquity as anyone else in history.

In 1933 he was created a Companion of Honour; in 1952 he became an Honorary Freeman of the Borough of Bermondsey.

His retirement from his various offices was so gradual as to be almost imperceptible, but in 1950 it was virtually complete, although he preached and attended committees almost to the very last. He died on 16th June 1953, within hailing distance of his ninety-ninth birthday.

THE METHODIST

CHAPTER ONE

THE METHODIST

WHEN Dr Scott Lidgett died in 1953 his admirers did not hesitate to acclaim him as the greatest Methodist since John Wesley. Such a judgement can be neither proved nor disproved; the significant thing is that it could be so confidently made and not seriously challenged.

In age and length of service his record has never been approached. He exercised an active ministry of seventy-three years, for no less than thirty-nine of which he was Chairman of one of the most important Methodist Districts. He was a link between the Methodism of the nineteenth and twentieth centuries, and for at least a generation was the greatest living repository of Methodist tradition. At the time of his Presidency of the Wesleyan Conference in 1908, he claimed to have been personally acquainted with fifty of the ninety-one Presidents who had occupied John Wesley's chair, and after that he was to live to see yet another forty-four holders of the office. When in 1946 the President died during his year of office, Dr Lidgett astonished his friends by describing the last occasion such an event had occurred, eighty-one years earlier.

While such longevity and years of service place Dr Lidgett in a category all his own, of themselves they do not justify the description, 'the greatest Methodist since John Wesley'. What those who made the claim had chiefly in mind was doubtless those qualities of mind and heart which Dr Lidgett possessed and the practical expression he gave to them in so many different forms of service, and it would perhaps be well for us, before we outline the details of that service, to notice some of those characteristics which support such a judgement and place him in the true line of Methodist succession.

This is all the more necessary when we realize that we are dealing with one who passed far beyond the limits of denominational recognition. Though exercising an active ministry of seventy-three years, he spent only fourteen of them as an itinerant Circuit minister, the other fifty-nine being devoted to the Bermondsey Settlement, where a wider public came to regard him as one of London's first citizens and one of our leading social reformers. The Free Churches came to claim him as in a very real sense belonging to them all, while in other quarters it was as a writer of theological books, and in yet others as a leading figure in the educational world in general and the University of London in particular, that he attained fame. If, in the light of all this, Methodists continue to claim him as peculiarly their own, it is due to their conviction that, in venerating this versatile servant of his fellows, the world, albeit unconsciously, is paying tribute to one who in all these various ways embodied Methodism at its best.

What, then, were some of those characteristics which marked Lidgett out as essentially a Methodist? It may be questioned whether any man in so many different ways has exemplified among his contemporaries and in the context of his own generation more of the outlook of Methodism's founder. Though it is not a point to labour, this was true of his own manner of life. Although such an outstanding man of affairs, Scott Lidgett was a man of personal austerity and plainness of speech. His was a simple piety and a single-minded devotion. Like Wesley, he disciplined his body to bear the strain of labours that would have broken the strength of an ordinary man. He had no interest whatever in his own material welfare, and through the years received no allowance as Warden of the Bermondsey Settlement. Absolutely free of the snare of self-seeking, he filled his mind with the thought of God and spent his strength in the redemptive service of his fellow men.

One of Wesley's claims for his Methodist followers was that they were the friends of all and the enemies of none. Such catholicity of outlook has surely never had a better exponent than Scott Lidgett. Tenacious of Free Church principles, he was yet the confidant of Archbishops. His autobiography tells how Archbishop Davidson during the greater part of his episcopate, whenever a question arose concerning the relation of religion and national life, would telephone the Bermondsey

Settlement and ask Lidgett to come to Lambeth and talk the matter over.[1]

This lifetime's work of promoting understanding and co-operation between the Churches received signal recognition toward the close of Dr Lidgett's life at a complimentary luncheon given in his honour on 5th October 1949, attended by many leaders in Church and State. Proposing Lidgett's health on that occasion, the Archbishop of Canterbury (Dr Geoffrey Fisher) said: 'It is perhaps symbolic of a good many things, and not least of Dr Lidgett's own work, that I, as Archbishop of Canterbury, should propose this toast and that I should be willing and glad to propose it. . . . Dr Lidgett remembers very well the bitter controversies that used to take place and the damage they did to the children and the Churches, but the position is very different now and I would say that not the least of this, if not the most, is due to Dr Scott Lidgett himself.' In the course of his reply Dr Lidgett said: 'In the forefront of my work has been the promotion of the Reunion of the Churches. The honour and the privilege came to me in 1913 of welcoming on behalf of the Free Church Council the representatives of the American Churches who came to stir up interest in this country in reunion. I introduced them to all the Churches—to Anglicans as well as the Free Churches—and then took part in bringing into existence the preparatory committee which prepared the way for the material proposals of the Lambeth Appeal in 1920. I worked in the closest intimacy with such Anglo-Catholics as Bishop Talbot and Bishop Gore and others, as well as with Evangelicals; and I may say to you that I found then an ecumenical atmosphere which made differences of Anglo-Catholics and even Baptists seem entirely out of place; for, say what we will and take whatever position we may, we belong to one another.'

Dr Lidgett expressed the hope that the President and the Archbishop would never retire one inch from the full programme for Reunion. 'Sectarianism is doomed', he declared in ringing tones, 'and neither heaven nor earth will have anything to do with it. The great keyword of our thought, our

[1] *My Guided Life*, p. 253.

sympathy and our practice, is catholicity; that we all belong to one another, and that whatever may have enriched our several denominations is not for the sake of the Anglican Church or the Methodist Church or any other Church, but for the enrichment in communion of us all. And so, my Lord Archbishop, I would like to see while I live the Lambeth Quadrilateral brought into full operation.'

He spoke of the inevitability of episcopacy being part of any scheme of Reunion, but it must be for him episcopacy 'under some conditions'. 'To begin with, I will not agree with any disparagement of that heroic mission of John and Charles Wesley which saved the English-speaking peoples of the world. In the next place, no one, I think, will be foolish enough to imagine that by a uniformity which would stereotype faith can a united Church be brought about. There must be recognition of the great traditions at the back of the Churches, springing from the root of the Apostles and the Primitive Church. They all took their rise from there. A truly catholic Church, to which all denominations can bring the riches of their inheritance—that is the ideal.'

But Lidgett was also catholic in another most important sense which emphatically places him in the true Wesleyan succession.

We have already noticed his single-mindedness. This was, however, linked with an astonishing versatility. Attaining distinction both as a theologian and as a man of affairs, this man of many parts was equally at home in the pulpit, on the platform, in the chair of a business meeting, or at a street corner addressing a heterogeneous crowd. Yet he was consistent throughout and, like St Paul, could justly declare: 'This one thing I do.' What was the secret? His own words afford the explanation. 'My theological interest has held the preference with me. I have always been engaged in expounding the Christian faith, particularly in its relation to practical life, convinced of the primacy of the fatherhood of God as revealed in Jesus Christ, in whom was realized the unity of human life, personal and social, spiritual and secular, ecclesiastical and national.'

Many of his friends lamented that so much of his working life was given to what seemed to them but a poor substitute for the books that he might have written, but to this Lidgett gave emphatic denial. 'From the outset of my career', he said, 'my main concern has been theological. So, far from my educational and other social activities having been a departure from this concern, they have been entirely based on my construction of what is involved in the Christian revelation of God and particularly in His fatherhood.'

It is generally recognized that an emphasis on 'Perfect Love' or 'Christian Holiness' as the end of all true religion is one of the main characteristics of John Wesley's teaching, which persisted from the 'Holy Club' days at Oxford until the end of his life. His evangelical conversion in 1738 in no way modified this emphasis, but rather showed him how it might be attained. In the last edition he himself published of his tract, *A Plain Account of Christian Perfection*, Wesley, now an old man, recalls his sermon on the subject preached before the University of Oxford in 1733 and remarks: 'This was the view of religion I then had, which even then I scrupled not to term "perfection". This is the view I have of it now, without any material addition or diminution.' Shortly before his death, Wesley referred to it in a letter thus: 'This doctrine is the grand depositum which God has lodged with the people called Methodists; and for the sake of propagating this chiefly He appeared to have raised us up.'

As understood by Wesley, however, the pursuit of holiness was never allowed to degenerate into pious religiosity. The atmosphere of the 'holiness sect' would have been repugnant to him. He was delivered from this by his insistence that true holiness must find constant expression in practical activity and especially in personal relationships. His own example in ministry to those in prison, his pioneer work in the field of education, and his passionate determination to preach the Gospel to the unprivileged, afford abundant testimony to this. Methodism at its best remained true to this heritage. Here is how one of its foremost nineteenth-century theologians expounded the practical side of holiness. 'Entire sanctification means the sanctification of everything. The sanctification, for example, of the daily work; that is, doing it to the Lord and, therefore, doing it as well as we can. If a ploughman be entirely sanctified, he will plough a straight furrow—or at least try his best to do so. If he be a mason, he will put no bad work into his wall; if a doctor, he will care more about curing his patients than about getting large fees; if he be a minister of religion, he will strive to serve the people of his charge to the utmost of his ability. . . . Entire sanctification means simply this: spending all our time in the Lord's service; making our religion our life, our life our religion.'[2]

Moreover, it is a commonplace that in the economic field it was the influence of the evangelical revival which carried the humanity of Christ out from the Church, so that, however unacknowledged has been its source, it has become the outstanding concern of statesmen. It has been the Christian witness that has awakened and inspired the social conscience of these later times. The Labour movement, we are rightly assured, owed more to Methodism than Marxism, and it was the former which gave the initial impetus to a process of which we see the latest fruits in the blessings of the Welfare State.

Dr Lidgett's own life is a great illustration of this. Cradled in the faith and experience of Methodism, he realized that the ultimate source of social progress lies in Christian theology. Out of this realization came the decision, in 1887, to offer to God the surrender of all his cherished ambitions of scholarship and teaching. This was the decision which led to the establishment of the Bermondsey Settlement.

Lidgett sought out the most neglected and poverty-stricken area of London and was told it was Bermondsey. In this choice he was doubtless influenced by Wesley's celebrated maxim: 'Go always not only to those that want you but to those that want you most.' Here, as the pioneering work developed and included ever wider interests within its range, he discovered, as he himself recounted again and again, that, in serving Bermondsey, he received back from God in fuller measure all he had renounced, and through his theological, educational, and social work, was able to carry out all he had thought he would for ever have to relinquish.

[2] Benjamin Hellier (*Life*, edited by his son and daughter), pp. 311f.

Here, then, was a man whose mind was filled with the thought of God while his hands were ever busy in the redemptive service of men. For him religious truth was not truth about religion but truth about life. Persuaded that all social progress was rooted in religion, he worked ceaselessly for every man's complete salvation—body, mind, and spirit. In an outstanding way he himself embodied the theory he proclaimed. His social enthusiasm was but an outward expression of his deep spirituality. He recognized the absolute obligation of righteousness over every conscience, calling on others as he strove himself to 'do all to the glory of God'.

In the light of these considerations, whatever we may feel about the aptness of the description, 'the greatest Methodist since John Wesley', there will scarcely be any disagreement with the verdict that of all the successors in Wesley's chair no name deserves to stand higher than that of John Scott Lidgett.

EARLY LIFE

On his father's side, Scott Lidgett was a Methodist of the third generation. Both his paternal grandparents were brought up in the Church of England, but became Methodists in early youth. His grandfather, John Lidgett, was a seafaring man, and was brought to a religious decision through the influence of 'Daddy' Post, a Methodist gate-keeper at the Hull Docks. John Lidgett rose quickly to the command of a vessel and, returning to the Port of London after one of his voyages, met his future wife, who had herself come to London from her home in Gloucester as a result of the opposition she encountered at home through becoming a Methodist.

On his mother's side, Lidgett's Methodist ancestry goes farther back. His grandfather, whose name he bore, was John Scott, one of the most eminent Wesleyan ministers of the day. John Scott's mother had heard Wesley preach, and he himself entered the Wesleyan Ministry in 1811. He was a trusted friend of the celebrated Dr Jabez Bunting and was twice President of the Conference. It would appear that his grandfather Scott was the most powerful single influence in Lidgett's early days. He always spoke and wrote about him with the deepest respect, and it is significant that in the changed circumstances of a later generation Lidgett himself filled a similar role to that of his distinguished grandfather. John Scott was involved in every aspect of Methodist life and policy, and sought to exercise a moderating influence in the 1849 controversies. His chief title to fame, however, was in the realm of education. This was the pioneering period of Wesleyan activity in this field. John Scott was Chairman of the Connexional Education Committee for twenty-five years after its formation in 1843. He was primarily responsible for the establishment of Westminster Training College for Teachers in 1851 and was its first Principal. It was fitting that his grandson, John Scott Lidgett, so worthy a successor to his grandfather in the educational field, should take part in 1951 in the centenary celebrations of the college, for the founding and early days of which John Scott had been so largely responsible.

John Scott's wife, Maria, was the daughter of a Sheffield manufacturer and had been a favourite of Dr Adam Clarke. Added to these memories was the continuous experience of meeting the leading Methodists of the day during her residence at Westminster, so that she was a veritable storehouse of information concerning Methodism's leading figure in the early years of the nineteenth century, which she constantly recounted for the benefit of her grandchildren.

Scott Lidgett's father, John Jacob Lidgett, died when his son was only fourteen years of age, but already he had achieved success in business and was becoming recognized as one who would make a notable contribution as a layman to Methodism. His mother lived to a great age and helped to found what eventually became known as the Women's Work of the Methodist Missionary Society, of which she became President.

It will thus be seen that Scott Lidgett was born and brought up in the inner circle of Methodism. He records that as an infant he was carried to receive the blessing of Dr Bunting as he lay on his death-bed. The homes of both his grandfathers and his father were centres to which most of the leading Methodists of the day came. He grew up in the Wesleyan Methodist Church at Blackheath, where the liturgical tradition of worship was faithfully maintained, and at an early age began to play his part in the worship and general life of the Church, receiving his first Communion when only thirteen years of age in January 1868 at the Covenant Service in Blackheath Chapel at the hands of his grandfather, John Scott, on the day before that veteran was struck down by a fatal attack of paralysis.

It is required of candidates for the Methodist Ministry that they should have already proved themselves in Church work, and during his years of adolescence Scott Lidgett's leisure was largely devoted to this. The Circuit to which he belonged included a Mission at East Greenwich, largely carried on by members of the Blackheath Society, whose enterprising minister, the Rev. George Bowden, organized a scheme of practical service to help the Mission. At the age of fifteen Scott Lidgett became a Sunday-school teacher at East Greenwich, where he raised funds to equip the schoolroom as a Wesleyan Day School. At East Greenwich also the following year he preached his first sermon, thereby taking the initial step toward becoming a local preacher, a necessary qualification for all who contemplate entering the Ministry. He himself narrates how, having embarked on a theological theme with great trepidation, he opened his Bible at the first chapter of Jeremiah and read the encouraging words: 'Thou therefore gird up thy loins, and arise, and speak unto them all that I command thee: be not dismayed at their faces, lest I confound thee before them' (verse 17). Thus fortified, he came satisfactorily through the ordeal and in due course was placed on the Circuit Plan. Meanwhile, Mr Bowden had been succeeded at Blackheath by the Rev. Samuel Coley, later theological tutor at Headingley College, from whom Lidgett received regular theological instruction on Saturday evenings. Finally, in 1872 Mr Coley conducted Lidgett's examination before the Circuit Local Preachers' Meeting. It was a hot June night and the examination took two hours, during which examiner and candidate together explored the intricacies of the Nicene controversy. At the end of it Scott Lidgett became a fully-fledged local preacher.

On joining the Church in 1868, Lidgett attended his uncle's

society class for a number of years, but at the age of eighteen Mr Coley appointed him a Class Leader, which meant that he met a small group of young men week by week and gave them religious advice and guidance.

When he was twenty, he left East Greenwich and assumed the superintendency of the Blackheath Sunday-school in somewhat remarkable circumstances. The previous Superintendent, in an attempt to enforce discipline on the older boys, had been set upon and knocked down by them. He summoned a policeman to help him to restore order, but made no subsequent appearance. The next Sunday Scott Lidgett took charge. Order prevailed and in the course of a few months the numbers in the school were trebled.

Even in those early days coming events cast their shadows before, and Lidgett's activities extended beyond the normal forms of Church work already described. He took responsibility, for example, for the distribution of tracts in an overcrowded court in East Greenwich, where, top-hatted as the fashion then was, he used to go straight from business on Saturday afternoons. At the same time he began open-air preaching, taking his stand by the gates of Greenwich Park and later outside the church, where he sought, often with success, to persuade passers-by to attend the evening service. With the co-operation of a local Anglican clergyman he raised money to erect a shelter for the cabmen on the rank in Blackheath, who up to that time had been entirely unprotected from the winds and rain which swept over that bleak spot.

In later life he described the Methodists of that mid-Victorian period as a people of simple dignity, unworldliness, and saintliness. The best of the ministers were well informed as to current movements of thought and on current affairs, but the implications of the new doctrine of evolution had at that time hardly made itself felt by them. Higher criticism had scarcely then been born; hence simple and unquestioning exposition of and insistence on the evangelical doctrines of Methodism formed the staple of their pulpit teaching, as it also expressed their individual belief. At the same time, in a significant way, the outlook of these Methodists was sharply divided from that of the evangelicals of the Church of England. The Methodist attitude both to political and social issues was altogether broader and more sympathetic to the advance of secular education and to social reforms.

Scott Lidgett's call to the Ministry came in the year 1870 when he was sixteen years old. At the close of his school career he had a great ambition to be a barrister (and what an advocate he would have made!). But one Sunday, at a morning service in the old Wesleyan chapel in Whitby, he listened to a sermon on the text, 'Son of man, I have made thee a watchman unto the house of Israel: therefore hear the word at my mouth, and give them warning from me' (Ezekiel 3[17]). The identity of the preacher was unknown, even to Lidgett himself, and they never met again. But the message went right home, and from that moment Lidgett never had any doubt that he was called to the Ministry of the Wesleyan Methodist Church. Not for a single moment did his conviction waver that he was separated for the work of the Ministry by his Lord and Saviour.

Lidgett's father had died a year or two before, and he was largely under the care of his uncle, George Lidgett. In the following autumn, therefore, with much shy hesitation, he informed his uncle and also his mother of this call which he felt he must obey. His uncle had already insisted on Lidgett's giving up his work in the classical sixth of the Blackheath Proprietary School to go into the City, with a view to a business career and eventually a partnership in the family business. Lidgett's newly-found sense of vocation only strengthened his uncle's determination to give him a business training, which, he believed, would prove an admirable test of the authenticity of his call and in any event would give him an experience of the world which would be a great advantage to a future minister. So Lidgett spent the next two years in the office of a firm of shipping and insurance brokers. When his decision to offer for the Ministry remained unshaken, he was at last permitted to enter University College, London, in January 1873, where he spent the next two and a half years, taking first the B.A. degree and then proceeding to the M.A. degree in

Logic and Philosophy. His father had originally intended that he should go to Oxford or Cambridge, but this his uncle resolutely opposed on the ground that such surroundings would not be likely to strengthen and might indeed undermine his Methodist convictions and sympathies. We may express our doubts on this point.

In 1875 Lidgett was introduced to Dr W. B. Pope, author of the celebrated *Compendium of Theology*, published during that year. For the next six years Pope was one of the great formative influences on Lidgett's thought. He had been taken by his uncle to Sheffield when the Conference was meeting. The young man was permitted to attend the Committee of Review. Up to that time the membership of the Conference had been confined to ministers, and Lidgett heard the famous speech of Mr Henry Fowler (afterwards Viscount Wolverhampton) in favour of lay representation. To the end of his life he retained a vivid recollection of the alarmed looks and apprehensive comments of some of the venerable divines. Dr Pope took him for a walk in the streets of Sheffield and counselled the young student to spend the next year in studying Biblical Theology, prescribing Isaiah in Hebrew and the Epistle to the Galatians in Greek. That the greatest of Methodism's dogmatic theologians should have given such advice at such a time is significant in view of the renewed emphasis placed on Biblical Theology in our own day. Lidgett's other trusted adviser and friend from this time forward was Dr William F. Moulton, first headmaster of the newly-founded Leys School at Cambridge.

In 1876 Lidgett was accepted as a candidate for the Ministry. Being already a graduate, and additional ministers being in great demand, he was not sent to a theological college but was accepted for what is called 'Home immediate'. While he was undoubtedly well equipped for this, better indeed than most, it did mean that he missed the opportunity which would have been given by college life of forming intimate friendships with his ministerial contemporaries. It was, therefore, for him an unusually violent transition from the life of a university and the environment of a respectable suburban church to the excitable and emotional religious atmosphere of the industrial town of

Tunstall in the Potteries, to which Circuit he was first appointed. For the story of Lidgett's ministry so long ago we are almost entirely dependent on his own written reminiscences, but we may assume that, if his new surroundings were strange to him, his advent was also a somewhat novel experience for his congregations. At any rate, one school teacher in Tunstall walked three miles on the first Sunday morning in September to see and hear this unusual phenomenon, a newly appointed young Wesleyan minister with an M.A.!

Methodism was, for all practical purposes, the established religion of the Potteries at that time. In Tunstall there were flourishing Wesleyan churches in the town itself, while there were about a dozen societies in the colliery villages round about. It had been the original mission of Methodism to evangelize the great industrial population springing up everywhere as a result of the industrial revolution. The State had not yet awakened to its responsibilities for educating the people, and in consequence elementary education was almost entirely provided by denominational schools. There was a large Wesleyan day school in Tunstall, and others in most of the surrounding villages; the teachers were largely old students of John Scott.

His work proceeded on the normal lines of a Circuit minister. The mornings were devoted to study, the afternoons to pastoral visitation, and the evenings to week-night preaching-services in the various villages. He has given us two or three glimpses of incidents in which he was involved. In one particularly dreary village he arranged an annual flower show. On one occasion he found himself involved in an evangelistic mission, one of a series arranged throughout the country at the suggestion of the then President of the Conference. The mission took the form of a week of special services in Tunstall at which the local ministers were to take turns in helping the missioner by taking charge of the after-meeting in an 'inquiry room'. On the first night Lidgett returned from a village service to find an excited and noisy gathering, hopelessly out of the control of the minister in charge. The next night it was Lidgett's turn to preside and he determined there should be no repetition of this scene. As each noisy person came into the inquiry room, conducting young people who had responded to the appeal, Lidgett allotted them vacant places and gave strict instructions to each helper that he must give only whispered advice, so that the new converts might understand the seriousness of the step they had taken. Whenever noisy ejaculations broke out, Lidgett either announced a hymn or called on the interrupter to offer prayer. So excitement was held in check and order prevailed.

On another occasion, bored by the appalling solemnity of a Sunday-school Anniversary meeting with endless recitations and addresses, Lidgett asked the chairman to be allowed to offer a prize. Consent being obtained, he called on the boys to range themselves round several iron pillars which supported the roof of the building and at his signal swarm up them as quickly as possible. This incident suggests that in a later age Scott Lidgett would have been a resourceful Youth Club Leader.

After two years in the Tunstall Circuit Lidgett was removed, at the instance of Dr Pope, to the newly founded Southport (Mornington Road) Circuit. It would have been difficult to conceive a greater contrast in environment and type of work than that which Southport provided. The population consisted largely of wealthy businessmen from Liverpool, Manchester, and other Lancashire towns, who resided in Southport or who had retired to that resort in their declining years. Lidgett felt it in many ways deplorable that the work and influence of these people were thus withdrawn from the industrial centres where their wealth had been made and where their workpeople still lived. It was yet another aspect of the social problem of the day brought about by the Industrial Revolution, and it both oppressed and impressed him. The need to bring together such extremes profoundly exercised his mind. In its own way Southport Methodism was as flourishing as that of the Potteries, and Lidgett spent his time preaching to large congregations, conducting Bible classes and visiting his people. Here, too, there were many schools, though of a different character from those in Tunstall. Southport has always been a favourite place for private schools and Lidgett found many opportunities of serving them. During this period, too, he was an unremitting student, spending an average of five to seven hours a day in his study.

Little else is known of the Southport ministry, but after the normal term of three years Lidgett was moved to the Cardiff (Wesley) Circuit, a sphere he found much more congenial. The Welsh city was steadily approaching the height of its commercial prosperity, and its energy and enterprise in business and civic life made a strong appeal to Lidgett. He found it much easier than in Southport to enlist the services of young people in various forms of social service, such as giving regular concerts to the inmates of the workhouse. The Wesleyan Church, too, occupied a leading place in the religious life of the community. Among other activities Lidgett in his first year there raised the money to build a new church in a rapidly growing working-class area. He also took a prominent part in the Blue Ribbon Temperance movement, and was organizing secretary of the great Moody and Sankey mission in the autumn of 1882. While in no way sharing Moody's fundamentalist outlook in theology, Lidgett was deeply impressed by the humility, the sound common sense and the consuming religious passion of the evangelist. During his Cardiff ministry Lidgett became closely associated with Dr Charles J. Vaughan, Dean of Llandaff and Master of the Temple. Among other things, Vaughan and Lidgett helped to persuade the Town Council to include in its Municipal Bill, for submission to Parliament, clauses dealing with the disorderly houses, which constituted a grave scandal at the time in the dock area. They were also instrumental, in the spring of 1883, following a visit to the town of Miss Ellice Hopkins of the White Cross Society, in founding a Preventive Home for Girls. This home still exists, its management having been transferred to the Committee of the National Children's Home.

In Cardiff Lidgett met, and at the end of his ministry there married, the lady who shared his fortunes for nearly half a century. She was Emmeline Martha, the second daughter of a well-known physician, Dr Andrew Davies, who was an active member of the Church of England, while his wife was a devoted Wesleyan Methodist.

In 1884 came a move to Wolverhampton, where Lidgett was stationed at Heath Town, a working-class district, with charge also of the neighbouring village of Wednesfield. In this Circuit Lidgett, in addition to the normal duties he was expected to discharge, found time to initiate schemes of educational and social work, including an early Sunday morning school for working men and a series of Saturday evening concerts and lectures. He also took a great interest in the Wesleyan Day School and organized recreative evening schools for boys and girls throughout the town. This most valuable pioneering experiment was part of a nation-wide scheme initiated by Dr J. B. Paton, Principal of the Congregational Theological College in Nottingham. Up to that time there was nothing done for children in the evenings, and they lived largely in the streets, with deplorable consequences. This work proved to be the forerunner of the system of Evening Continuation Schools which spread through the country.

Meanwhile Mrs Lidgett was busily engaged conducting women's societies, organizing annual flower shows and assisting her husband in his varied activities.

But perhaps Lidgett's most distinctive contribution in the Wolverhampton Circuit was the formulation and carrying through of a comprehensive scheme of chapel-building. Many of the smaller chapels in the poorer parts of the neighbourhood had fallen into disrepair and were inadequate in other ways, and with generous financial support from local friends and others Lidgett dealt with the buildings in order and carried the scheme to a successful conclusion during his three years' ministry.

In 1887 Lidgett moved from Wolverhampton to Cambridge, which was to be his last normal Circuit appointment. His special charge was the Hills Road Church, at that time attended by the masters and boys of The Leys School. Here again there was a scheme of church extension and improvement which required his attention, and here again he established recreative evening classes for the boys of the town, being supported on this occasion by some of the University dons, whose daughters also rendered active help.

How the call came to him in Cambridge to undertake what was to be his main life-work is described elsewhere. We may close this account of Lidgett's fourteen years of Circuit ministry by remarking on the unusual breadth of his experience. Tunstall, Southport, Cardiff, Wolverhampton and Cambridge afforded a variety of experience enjoyed by few. He responded with equal vigour and ability to the demands of each, and each in turn played its part in fitting him for the outstanding service he was to render with such distinction in many different fields. In 1890 he moved to Bermondsey, where he remained as Warden of the Settlement for fifty-nine years and from which he exercised an ever-increasing influence in Church and State.

Scott Lidgett was beginning to exert an influence throughout the Wesleyan Methodist Connexion while still a Circuit minister. In 1887 he attended the Conference for the first time as a representative, and after that year he rarely, if ever, missed. Being permanently resident in London from 1890 onward, he was in an advantageous position, and became an almost inevitable selection when committees on constitutional and public issues were appointed. He was made secretary of the Committee of Privileges, which in the Wesleyan Church was charged with the responsibility of taking action on all national occasions and in all matters affecting the interests, duties, rights or privileges of the Church. In 1902 he was elected by the Conference a member of the Legal Hundred. This body, composed exclusively of ministers, remained the legal Conference of the Wesleyan Methodist Church until Methodist Union in 1932, when it disappeared. At the close of the proceedings of the Conference each year, the Legal Hundred, by a standing vote, formally ratified all that had been done during the Conference, and only that ratification made those decisions effective. Membership of the Legal Hundred was a much coveted distinction, conferred on a minister as a mark of the confidence of his brethren.

But it was the year 1903 which, once for all, established Scott Lidgett's position in the Conference and the Church. Leadership of the progressive element in Wesleyan Methodism had in the immediately preceding years rested on the shoulders of Hugh Price Hughes, who died suddenly in November 1902. Up to that time Lidgett had kept himself somewhat aloof from questions of organization and Church policy. His time and energy were fully occupied with other matters and he had not felt attracted in that direction. On the night of Hughes's death Lidgett had been in his company, and it was a tremendous shock to him to learn early the next morning that Hughes was dead. He retired into seclusion for several hours, and there came over him an overwhelming conviction that henceforth he must undertake fresh responsibilities and play his part in ecclesiastical affairs. The following July he attended the Conference at Camborne under the constraint of a new sense of vocation. At the opening of the Conference what he himself describes as a 'momentous afflatus' came upon him.

The vital debate in the Conference concerned the great educational controversy which was raging at that time. The details of the controversy fall outside the scope of this chapter, but it was, of course, a theme on which Lidgett was well qualified to speak. When he rose to address the assembly he was lifted out of himself, and his speech made a tremendous impression and opened an altogether new chapter in his life. This is how the *Methodist Recorder* described it:

'Mr Scott Lidgett, declining to mount the platform, seconds the resolution. He speaks fluently and carries the Conference with him. An effective quotation from the late Archbishop Temple produces a great silence. The best argument against rate-aided, as distinguished from Imperial, taxation he had given. The whole question he then lifted out of the fractious and irritating atmosphere of political advocacy and consciously swayed the Conference. His handling of the rating and Passive Resistance resolution was effective in the extreme, and all the more effective because he plainly and courageously disavowed sympathy with Passive Resistance as a policy, while at the same time avowing sympathy with those who conscientiously refuse to pay rates. This undoubtedly is one of the greatest speeches ever delivered in the Conference during our times.'

Lidgett made other contributions to the deliberations that year, and, as their secretary, presented the reports of the Committee of Privileges and the Social Purity Committee. The following week it is recorded that in the Pastoral Session, when the Rev. George Denton, convener of the Committee of Scrutineers, presented the list of votes cast for the next year's President and read out, 'J. Scott Lidgett, six', there was a half-involuntary cheer. A coming event had cast its shadow before.

From 1903 to 1905 Lidgett was Chairman of the London Methodist Council, and in 1906 he assumed the editorship of the *Methodist Times*, the paper founded by Hugh Price Hughes on modern and aggressive lines. At first he hesitated to accept this post, being entirely unused to popular journalism, but eventually he yielded to the pressure brought to bear on him, and occupied the editorial chair of the paper until 1918, during which period he wrote leading articles weekly, except on two occasions, and also the greater part of the weekly notes on current affairs. Throughout he sought to make the paper the organ of a persistent progressive policy, contending for liberty of thought in Methodism, subject always to the preservation of the essential doctrines of the faith. Finally, the 1907 Conference designated him as President of the Wesleyan Methodist Conference, to which office he succeeded in 1908.

These early years of Lidgett's ministry coincided with a period of rapid transition in more than one sphere. We have already had cause to note the social effects of the Industrial Revolution and the consequent opportunities and challenges they afforded to the Church, and we have observed how Lidgett, more than any other one man in the Methodism of the day, save Hugh Price Hughes himself, responded to the challenge.

Equally critical, however, was the reaction of Methodism when confronted by another revolution—that which was taking place in modern thought. Lidgett has told of the unpleasant impression made on him as a young minister by events in 1880, when Dr W. H. Dallinger was to have delivered a Fernley Lecture, in which he proposed to accept and expound the doctrine of evolution in its relation to theism. The prevailing attitude of those who had to decide the matter was that the view was probably true but its expression was inopportune. The arrangement with Dr Dallinger was cancelled and another lecture substituted at the last moment, though the offending lecture was subsequently delivered seven years later in 1887.

Lidgett's own Fernley Lecture, *The Spiritual Principle of the Atonement*, almost met a similar fate in 1897. A proof copy was sent to the President of the Conference, Dr Marshall Randles, Theological Tutor at Didsbury College, accompanied by the allegation that in some important respects it was heretical. The President agreed, but fortunately no extreme action was taken.[3] Only five years later, in 1902, Dr Randles and Dr W. L. Watkinson supported Lidgett's nomination for the vacant Theological Chair at Richmond College, but Lidgett withdrew his name.

In ranging himself on the progressive side in the intellectual controversies of the day, Lidgett was a faithful disciple of his two mentors, W. B. Pope and W. F. Moulton; when the cause was won, he was able to declare that one of the most striking things about Methodism was that it had lived through the greatest transformation of human thought and the greatest increase of human knowledge in all fields known to history and that, having first opposed and then hesitated, it had come to accept the modern point of view and to find in that point of view the confirmation and enlargement, instead of the disturbance and destruction, of its faith. In that achievement he had played no small part.

Inevitably, however, he came to be regarded in some quarters as a dangerous person, and energetic efforts were made by those who viewed him with suspicion to postpone, if not to prevent, his election to the chair of the Conference. When, however, this opposition was overcome and he became President, the *Methodist Recorder*, in an article of appreciation, wrote thus:

'In him, more perhaps than in any other man, the progressive

---

[3] Lidgett's account of this incident is quoted, with a comment, on p. 86, *infra*.

forces of Methodism find their focus. He will probably prove a Young People's President. His interest in the Wesley Guild and in Sunday-school work, his position at the head of the Union for Social Service, his strong following among the younger ministers of the Church, his broad sympathy with all the forces of modern life, save those of wrong and reaction, will combine to give him the ear of younger Methodism as a few, but not many, of his predecessors have possessed it. His face is turned toward the future, and in more than one respect he is an embodiment of the Methodism that is to be—a Church broad as well as deep in her spirituality, refusing to put asunder those elements of life which God Himself has joined together. The spiritual part of our religion involves the theological; for right emotions cannot dispense with firm intellectual bases. And both the spiritual and the theological sides of our religion involve the social: for the spiritual claims expression in every relationship of human life, and the social principles which must govern that expression are only sure deductions from the profoundest and most treasured doctrines of our faith. It is in this unity of the religious life that Mr Scott Lidgett's teaching and personality find their chief significance.'

FIRST PRESIDENCY

Loyalty to the President of the Conference is recognized among Methodists as both a duty and a privilege. In spite, therefore, of the doubts and hesitations which had existed in some quarters, Scott Lidgett, when he was elected, received the sympathy and support of the whole Connexion. In many respects it proved to be a memorable Presidential year, which altogether fulfilled the high expectations of Lidgett's friends. He consistently emphasized at the Conference itself and in his utterances during the year the social and even the political responsibilities of the Church. He organized a series of conventions throughout the country which were well-attended and successful, and in this way his message reached not only the populous centres but also the country areas, through some of which he travelled on motor-tours arranged by the Chairmen of the Districts. Everywhere he stressed the social implications of Christian faith, relating these to Wesley's teaching on 'perfect love' as the ideal of true religion. He pursued the same policy at the Southport Holiness Convention, at a three-days' conference of the Union for Social Service, and at the Easter gathering of the recently established Wesley Guild. He persuaded the representatives of the Guild to commit their branches to clearing the debt then existing on the Foreign Missionary Society (as it was then called), thus giving the initial impetus to the missionary zeal of the Wesley Guild, which has since found its expression in the maintenance of the hospital at Ilesha in Nigeria. The President invited some of the younger ministers to accompany him on his visits, with the result that by the end of his year of office his point of view had become widely shared by the Church as a whole and its younger section in particular.

Lidgett himself relates how on the occasion of the Norwich convention, when large numbers came from all over East Anglia, the railway ran special excursions to the city and advertised the following list of attractions for the day:

> FAT CATTLE SHOW
> CHRYSANTHEMUM SHOW
> DOG AND KENNEL SHOW
> HIPPODROME—TWICE DAILY
> VISIT OF THE REV. J. SCOTT LIDGETT

Perhaps the most noteworthy single event of the year concerned the Licensing Bill which had been introduced in May 1908. The Conference in July, under Lidgett's Presidency, passed a strong resolution in its favour, with only eight dissentients. More than a million Wesleyans had signed a petition in favour of it. Instead, however, of the House of Lords according it a fair and full discussion, after it had passed the House of Commons, a party meeting outside the House resolved to reject the measure outright without amendment on its second reading. Lidgett regarded this as a direct challenge to the Churches by powerful vested interests. The news reached him just as he was about to address the great anniversary meeting of the Manchester Mission in the Free Trade Hall.

Forthwith he despatched a telegram to Lord Lansdowne, Conservative leader in the House of Lords, at whose home the private meeting had been held, to the effect that if the House of Lords rejected the Bill without discussing it the action 'would never be forgiven or forgotten by the Wesleyan Methodist Church'. He then announced the action to the assembled gathering and read the telegram, whereupon there followed a scene of tremendous enthusiasm, the whole audience rising and cheering frantically for several minutes. The usual outcry against the President of the Conference taking part in politics found some expression in the correspondence columns of the *Methodist Recorder*, but this only recoiled on the heads of the objectors and the correspondence was quickly closed.

These special activities all needed to be fitted into the arduous round of official engagements the President was expected to fulfil. At the end of the year not only was Lidgett firmly established in the confidence of the denomination, which he was to enjoy undiminished from that time forward, but, as a result of his advocacy, the Connexion as a whole had come to recognize with fresh insight the need for that continuous expression of the implications of the Gospel on the urgent social issues of the day, which has characterized the outlook of Methodism in recent times.

METHODIST UNION

During his lifetime John Wesley maintained an almost autocratic control over the Methodist societies. His ceaseless journeyings throughout the Connexion and his voluminous correspondence with all and sundry enabled him to keep in constant touch; in addition to which he always presided over the annual Conference, which was, in fact, the instrument of his will. After his death, however, when lesser men without his practical genius sought to govern the Connexion after the same fashion, it is hardly surprising that dissensions arose, some of which resulted in secessions from the main body. The two main cleavages took place in 1805 and 1849, the former of which led to the formation of the Primitive Methodist Church. There is no need to enter here into the details of the various controversies, save to say that each of these secessions was a revolt against the rigidity of the Wesleyan Methodist Church, and represented a demand for a more democratic constitution, and especially for a larger share for the laity in matters of Church government. With the passing years, however, the Wesleyan Church itself, albeit more slowly, became informed with a more democratic spirit, and we have already described how the purely ministerial government of the Church gave way eventually to a Conference of two sessions, the Representative Session, which included laymen, being followed by a Pastoral Session for the spiritual oversight of the Church and for the appointment and discipline of ministers. The first Representative Session was held in 1887.

The various secessions had all been caused by disputes about Church government and in no way affected the common faith and common mission of all the people called Methodists, so that when the time came that the main causes of disunion were no longer features of Wesleyan Methodism, the way was open for an approach to reunion, and it is significant that the first speech advocating it was made by Sir Robert Perks as soon as laymen had gained their place in the Wesleyan Conference. It is easier, however, to secede than to reunite, and it was thirty-five years before the first definite action was taken. During this period the *Methodist Times* kept the subject alive, first under Hugh Price Hughes, then under Scott Lidgett, who in 1904 proposed the holding of a Methodist Assembly in Wesley's Chapel to manifest the unity of Methodism in its doctrinal and evangelical faith. This assembly undoubtedly helped to further the cause of unity.

In 1907 three of the smaller Methodist denominations— the Methodist New Connexion, the Bible Christians, and the United Methodist Free Church—came together to form the United Methodist Church. Lidgett assisted the passage of the Bill through Parliament and, as a visitor at the first Conference, was among those who offered the congratulations of Methodism generally at the event. This union, by reducing the number of negotiating parties, helped greatly to pave the way for the next stage, as did the liberal spirit which increasingly characterized the policy of the Wesleyan Church after the admission of laymen to the Conference.

Eventually, the Wesleyan Conference of 1913 passed the following resolution: 'The Conference, in accepting the report of the Ecumenical Methodist Commission, expresses its profound gratitude at the increasing desire for unity among all the branches of the Methodist Church, and, being convinced that the time has come when a serious effort should be made to unite in one Church organization the different branches of British Methodism, the Conference appoints a Committee to collect information and report to the next Conference.'

The outbreak of war in 1914 held matters up somewhat, but the Conference of 1917 passed the following resolution: 'The Conference resolves that the Committee be enlarged, and empowers it to meet any Committees of the other British Methodist Churches so as to confer with them on these questions.'

Lidgett was not on the original committee but became a member of the enlarged committee in 1917, being present at its first meeting on 11th October of that year. A year later, in October 1918, we find him contributing to a discussion in the committee which stressed the importance of a thorough understanding with the other Churches as to the doctrine of the Pastoral Office and the Sacraments that would need to be laid down for the United Church before union could take place.

The following day he was present at the first meeting of the United Committee, including representatives of the three Churches appointed by the respective Conferences of 1918. That committee set up various sub-committees and Lidgett was among the Wesleyans appointed to the sub-committee to deal with constitutional questions.

From that time forward many sub-committees were appointed with specific tasks, and Lidgett figured prominently on many of them, besides exercising an ever-increasing influence on the main committee itself.

On 28th September 1920 we find him in the chair of the Publicity Committee appointed by the Executive, and the following year he took an active part in arranging the holding of United Meetings in accordance with the direction of the Conference.

Meanwhile, the scheme for reunion was being drafted and was submitted in due course to the Quarterly Meetings of the Churches for an expression of opinion.

In March 1925 the Executive appointed by the United Committee reviewed the figures of the voting at the December Quarterly Meetings of the three Churches, and Lidgett moved the following resolution: 'That, in view of the returns from the three Churches that have been presented, the United Committee be recommended to advise the several Conferences to declare that the majority in the Churches is sufficient to go forward with the proposal for reunion, on the basis of the scheme that has been submitted, according to their constitutional procedure, and that the Conferences be recommended to instruct the United Committee to consider and report as to the methods and stages by which reunion, if finally adopted, may be carried out with due regard to all the interests, central and local, that are concerned.'

In the event the Conferences of that year declared in principle in favour of union on the basis of the scheme, but remitted the matter to the Synods of 1926 to ascertain their views. The various committees were reappointed to continue discussions on points where there was not yet complete agreement, and were also instructed that a report should be made to the 1926 Conferences respecting the methods and stages by which Union, when finally agreed, might be carried out. It was also declared that at least seventy-five per cent. of each Session of the Conference in favour of the scheme should be required before seeking an Enabling Act.

The following November sub-committees were appointed by the Executive on various matters, one of the most important having as its business the reconsideration of the Doctrinal and Sacramental clauses in accordance with the resolution of the Conferences.

When this sub-committee met, Lidgett was in the chair, and it was resolved to appoint a yet smaller committee to draw up a doctrinal statement to replace the statement in the scheme. When this committee met, with Lidgett again presiding, an amended form of statement was submitted, which Lidgett and Dr A. S. Peake were asked to revise in preparation for the next meeting of the sub-committee.

This statement, which clearly owed much to Lidgett's powers of logical and concise expression, became and still is the doctrinal basis of the Methodist Church. It runs as follows:

'The Methodist Church claims and cherishes its place in the Holy Catholic Church, which is the Body of Christ. It rejoices in the inheritance of the apostolic faith, and loyally accepts the fundamental principles of the historic Creeds and of the Protestant Reformation. It ever remembers that in the providence of God Methodism was raised up to spread Scriptural holiness through the land by the proclamation of the evangelical faith, and declares its unfaltering resolve to be true to its divinely appointed mission.

'The doctrines of the evangelical faith, which Methodism has held from the beginning, and still holds, are based upon the divine revelation recorded in the Holy Scriptures. The Methodist Church acknowledges this revelation as the supreme rule of faith and practice. These evangelical doctrines, to which the preachers of the Methodist Church, both Ministers and Laymen, are pledged, are contained in Wesley's *Notes on the New Testament* and the first four volumes of his *Sermons*.

'The *Notes on the New Testament* and the *Forty-four Sermons* are not intended to impose a system of formal or speculative theology on Methodist preachers, but to set up standards of preaching and belief which should secure loyalty to the fundamental truths of the gospel of redemption, and ensure the continual witness of the Church to the realities of the Christian experience of salvation.'

From this time forward the project developed according to plan, with Lidgett regularly present at the important committees and often in the chair. In October 1926 he presided over a sub-committee to prepare plans for the unification of the Districts and Synods.

In the autumn of 1927 he presided over and took an active

part in the meeting of a Business Committee appointed by the Wesleyan Conference.

Finally, in 1928, the requisite majorities in favour of Union were obtained in all the Conferences, and preparations set afoot to consummate the Union in 1932. Innumerable committees met dealing with such matters as legal procedure, codification of regulations, and so on, and Lidgett was a dominating figure throughout. Many of those who had played a prominent part in the earlier negotiations had died, and it was a recognition of the unique place which was now his in Methodism, and British Christianity in general, as well as of his share in the actual union negotiations, that he was the inevitable choice as the first President of the reunited Methodist Church in 1932.

When the intimation of this crowning distinction came to him his word was: 'Brethren, pray for me.'

It has been no part of our intention in this chapter to give a detailed account of the prolonged negotiations which eventually issued in Methodist Union, a story which would fill a volume in itself, but rather to indicate Lidgett's part in them, which, though small at first, became steadily larger as the years went by.

When, shortly after Union, Lidgett was presented for the degree of Doctor of Divinity at Oxford, he was described by the Public Orator of the University as 'the principal author of the recent union of the three Methodist Churches'.

This judgement will hardly command universal assent. Names of others will occur to the reader, who with Lidgett could justly be claimed as joint architects of the scheme. It may be fairly said, however, that no other individual exercised a greater influence, and that, if in those critical years when his stature was steadily increasing he had been an opponent of the policy instead of a consistent advocate, it is doubtful whether Union would have been achieved. This, however, is to suggest the impossible. Such an attitude would have been a denial of all he stood for, not least of his view of Methodism, which he once described as 'a most remarkable enshrining of Apostolic and Catholic truth in a living Evangelic experience'. As such, Methodism, he believed, was presented with an immense opportunity of serving the universal Church and the nation in this crisis of their history. Furthermore, Methodism at its best, when true to its heritage, had always proclaimed the unity of spiritual and social concerns in a complete Christian faith and outlook. Its ability to discharge the responsibilities laid on it in the Providence of God must not be hampered by differences within itself about authority and ecclesiastical organization. The outstanding 'catholic' of his day could not but be an ardent supporter of Methodist Union.

CHAIRMAN OF THE DISTRICT

The Chairman of a District occupies a key position in Methodism. Technically, his duties are relatively few. He presides over the District Synod in September and May, and over the District Committees held in preparation for the Synod. He is also responsible for discipline within the District. In fact, however, he does very much more. He represents the District in Connexional matters and interprets the mind of the Connexion to the circuits and churches. By virtue of his office he is an ex-officio member of the Conference and of the Connexional Home Mission Committee. Though not of constitutional necessity, he is almost invariably the ministerial representative of his Synod on the Connexional General Purposes Committee and the Stationing Committee. Thus he is in the inner councils of the Church and at the same time in continuous touch with the ministers and laymen throughout his District. If he wins their confidence, his influence is paramount.

Lidgett's election to the chair of the Wesleyan Conference in 1908 placed him in the chair of the Third London District, which after Methodist Union became in effect the London South District. He occupied the position for no less than thirty-nine years, a record never approached by any other minister.

Though not what is called a separated Chairman, that is a Chairman with no other pastoral responsibilities, his post during the whole period as Warden of the Bermondsey Settlement left him free from normal Circuit duties, and thus he was able to devote a good deal of time to the District. This he did with unswerving devotion, and of the many responsibilities which claimed his time and energies none lay nearer his heart. When presented with his portrait at a District gathering toward the end of his chairmanship, he said: 'I love you people in the South London District better than any other people in the world.'

His friend, the Rev. J. Edwin Reding, who was for many years the Secretary of the Synod and eventually succeeded Lidgett in the chair, has kindly given me some impressions and recollections of Lidgett in his capacity as Chairman.

He was a most dominating and alert Chairman of the Synod. While there were those who found him autocratic, all recognized his great gifts of statesmanship and the authority with which he could speak on all questions concerning not only the Methodist Church but all the Churches. There were those who thought him too aloof and stern, judging him by his peremptory and sometimes devastating asides in the conduct of the business of the Synod. Because of this, some men would not speak freely or even feel at ease in his presence. But all honoured and respected him, and were inspired and instructed by his speeches. There were those who did not know how much kindness, goodwill and human sympathy there was in his character. To those of his friends who had been bereaved he was a true comforter. He had himself suffered and travelled the road of suffering. And when he prayed there was awe in his voice and the whole assembly felt the presence of God.

Lidgett belonged to a generation which practised austerity in ministerial dress and deportment. He never himself abandoned this and, though far too great a man to attach undue importance to so secondary a matter, the following incident would suggest that he looked askance at the laxity of some of his younger brethren. He was passing one of the young ministers when he heard himself addressed: 'Good morning, Doctor.'

'Who are you?' he inquired.

'I am so-and-so, a minister in your District.'

Lidgett glanced at the young man, lightly garbed and with soft collar and coloured tie, and replied: 'Oh, are you? Then all I can say is you are suffering from ecclesiastical nudity. Good morning.'

There was also the brother who was talking over much in

the Synod and to little purpose. Lidgett's patience gave out, and turning to the Secretary he said in a voice which could be heard beyond the platform: 'Well, it is time that this man became a supernumerary.' He himself was eighty-eight at the time and still in full work.

During the years of the second World War he called together the superintendents of Circuits and their stewards to record the damage to their church premises. He listened for more than an hour and then dictated several pages of particulars concerning war-damaged buildings. Once he was interrupted; turning to the minister who had intervened, he said: 'Don't interrupt; can't you see I am thinking?' He omitted nothing and added nothing. When congratulated afterwards, he said with a chuckle: 'Thank you, I have had much practice in these things.'

It seems doubtful whether he would ever have retired voluntarily, but the time came when, in spite of their unbounded affection and respect, some members of the Synod began to feel that a younger man should succeed to the office, and year by year an increasing number of votes were cast accordingly. Most men would have regarded this as a warning signal and would have taken the hint. But not so Lidgett, and it was only when the majority of the Synod voted for Mr Reding, though the Doctor had given no indication of his desire to be relieved, that he finally handed over the reins. It is easy to interpret this as wilful obstinacy, but that would be wrong. With his deep sense of constitutional propriety, Lidgett was perfectly willing for others to decide, in accordance with their right and duty so to do, when the time for a change had arrived. So long as it was physically possible and they were willing he was ready and eager to serve: when they decided otherwise, he accepted the verdict with complete humility and Christian grace. It was characteristic that, far from regarding this event as a dismissal, one of his remarks was: 'Now I must build my life afresh.'

On the day in the May Synod when for the last time he presided over its business as Chairman, he made one of his greatest and most moving speeches—as always, perfectly phrased. In strong and moving tones, he spoke of his long ministry in South London. His chief concern in that hour was not for himself, but for the District, the people, and the work to which his life had been devoted. He finished his speech by commending his successor to their prayers and co-operation, and within a few hours was asking Mr Reding for permission to preside at the Bermondsey Settlement committees.

LATER YEARS

Lidgett became President of the Wesleyan Conference just before his fifty-fourth birthday, at the zenith of his powers. For nearly another half century he was a trusted elder statesman.

It is somewhat surprising that he never took a prominent part in the councils of World Methodism. Many invitations to the United States had to be declined because of the pressure of multifarious duties at home. His only trip across the Atlantic was in 1911 when he attended the Ecumenical Methodist Conference in Toronto. It is significant, however, that on that occasion he was entrusted with the composition of the Encyclical Letter which the Conference sent out to be read in Methodist churches throughout the world at the beginning of the following year.

None who heard him will forget his mastery in Conference debate. There was the historic occasion when an appointment to Wesley's Chapel was under consideration. A well-known and popular minister was suggested for the appointment and the proposal commanded considerable support, especially among the younger men. Others were as definitely opposed, and feeling ran high. Lidgett's contribution undoubtedly decided the issue, and although in the light of later events his judgement on the matter may well be questioned, the incident well illustrated the power of his persuasive eloquence.

In later years he developed a hitherto unsuspected vein of humour, which he employed with great effect. Toward the end of his Conference career, he found himself on the opposite side to his great friend, Dr F. Luke Wiseman, perhaps the only senior minister in the Conference at that time whose influence could be compared to Lidgett's own. The question at issue was that of dancing on church premises. On this occasion

Lidgett supported the progressive viewpoint, and convulsed the Conference with a graphic description of himself taking the floor with an elderly lady of about his own age. 'As far as I know,' he concluded, 'we neither of us came to any harm.' The opposition crumpled and the cause was won.

The following description of Lidgett in debate will commend itself to all who heard him:

'As great conceptions came to birth, he saw them in their completeness as well as in the details of their component parts. He would begin a sentence, and then diverge into so many subordinate clauses that to everyone but himself it seemed clear that he was irretrievably lost in an impenetrable jungle, but he had them all under control. With unerring and flawless accuracy he moved on to the predestined conclusion, not, sometimes, without a small indication of satisfaction as he saw his audience release with relief the breath it had been holding while it waited for confusion to collapse into chaos.'

With his vision and outlook, he was bound to be deeply interested in Methodism's world mission and he was a constant friend of the cause of Overseas Missions. In 1935 the 'Anonymous Donor' who had been vastly generous in the past indicated that Methodism must henceforth give to the Missionary Society the support which until then he had given, which meant that the Society was faced with a considerable debt and the prospect of immediate retrenchment in the field. Dr Lidgett, in this extremity, wrote a vigorous letter to the *Methodist Recorder* to the effect that 'This must not be', and thanks to his leadership and energy, the entire debt was cleared in six months and retrenchment avoided. It is doubtful whether any other man could have so roused the Connexion.

Though by no means slow to detect it in others, he appeared quite oblivious of his own increasing years. In 1946 the Conference was held in London, and as the senior London Chairman (he was then ninety-two), he presided over the Conference Arrangements Committees and did not hesitate to rebuke men for not speaking clearly, when his own deafness was the cause of the trouble.

The well-known story of the artist is typical. When he had completed his portrait of Lidgett at the age of seventy-five, the artist, a much younger man, said to him: 'Doctor, I should like to paint you when you reach your hundredth birthday.' Lidgett, looking him up and down, replied: 'Well, I don't see why you shouldn't; you look quite strong and healthy.'

The last great public occasion at which Lidgett spoke was the service in commemoration of John and Charles Wesley, held in the University Church at Oxford during the World Methodist Conference of 1951. Lidgett was then ninety-seven years of age. A chair was provided for him near the reading-desk, from which he commanded a view of the crowded assembly. He insisted on standing for the recitation of the Creed and then preached for forty minutes. At the end he collapsed into unconsciousness. What an appropriate and triumphant ending it would have been for him to die preaching as a Methodist minister in the very church from which John Wesley had been banned! But a doctor was in attendance and succeeded in restoring him. On regaining full consciousness, he is said to have remarked: 'It is always said that preaching, if it is real preaching, ought to take it out of a man.'[4]

So he was spared a little time longer, during which he continued to attend those committees in which he was most interested.[5]

A few months before his death in 1953 he asked the present writer: 'Is it true, young man, that Conference is to come to London in 1954?' On being assured that it was indeed so, his eyes lighted up as he said: 'That will be my centenary year.' Had he lived, there can be little doubt that he would have been present to give his blessing. But it was not to be, and the end came just before the Conference of 1953, and with it the turning of a page in the history of Methodism.

ERIC W. BAKER

[4] He was already becoming conscious as he was lowered on to a stretcher, and remarked: 'facilis descensus.' He did not add, as Vergil did, Averno ('to the lower regions').—ED.

[5] At the last meeting of the Faith and Order Committee which he attended, in November 1952, he asked his neighbour, 'Who's that old man over there?' He was told, and commented; 'My, how old he's looking!' The 'old man over there' was a noted theologian more than thirty years his junior.—ED.

THE WARDEN OF THE BERMONDSEY SETTLEMENT

CHAPTER TWO

THE WARDEN OF THE BERMONDSEY SETTLEMENT

THERE is something noteworthy and arresting in the number one hundred. A century of sonnets attracts the attention as a mere score would not; and even if a hundred is 'soon hit', it counts for very much more than four score and ten. A hundred years, whatever their starting-point, gain a certain character of their own; and although the attainment of the allotted space of three score years and ten for a man's life calls for no special remark, the centenarian still enjoys his claim to royal notice.

It sometimes happens that the life of a single man stretches almost from end to end of some period of a hundred years which have been fruitful of changes in the history of society; and when the centenarian has himself been concerned to a greater or less extent in these changes, his record may well deserve more than a passing memory. Only seldom, however, has an individual's life spread over a hundred years at once pregnant and fertile; still less often has the long-lived individual seemed typical not merely of some aspect of the hundred years through which he has lived, but of the whole of their ample sweep. Though he died just before completing his own hundred years, this is what marks the career of John Scott Lidgett.

Born in 1854, and living till 1953, he saw the beginning and the end of a century which has itself seen greater changes in the life of this country, in whatever quarter we choose to look for them, than any other which could be easily named. And when we consider those changes more carefully, we shall sooner or later find ourselves meeting Scott Lidgett, and even (such is at least the opinion of the writers of this book) recognizing his hand and his thought in nearly all of them. It has been given to few to play such a part, and indeed such a conspicuous part, in so long a chain of notable events.

J. R. Green would find the turning-point from the old to the new more than a hundred years earlier: 'The England that is about us' (he is writing in 1874), 'dates from the American War. It was then that the moral, the philanthropic, the religious ideas which have moulded English society into its present shape first broke the spiritual torpor of the eighteenth century.' G. M. Trevelyan is inclined to agree: the first fifty years from the War of Independence to the Reform Bill 'compose a single epoch'. In spite of the miseries which culminated between Waterloo and Peterloo, we had Cowper, Burns, Blake, Coleridge, and Wordsworth, the activities of the Clapham Sect, and the founding of the British and Foreign Bible Society. Professor Gilbert Murray calls attention to a factor which is often overlooked even by judicious historians: 'The Evangelical Revival had led to a new doctrine of responsibility to the non-privileged.' But future historians may find ample reasons for seeing that movements and convictions with which previous generations were big came to birth together in the middle of the last century. What new births will follow in the next hundred years from now we must leave posterity to discover; but whatever they are, they will be dealt with more intelligently through some knowledge of the times of Scott Lidgett, and of his own life.

We are not usually accustomed, when dealing with the nineteenth or twentieth centuries, to attribute much social or national influence to ministers of religion. We look most naturally to statesmen and administrators. But the influence of statesmen as a factor in the life of a nation may easily be exaggerated. 'What shadows we are,' cried one of the greatest of them; 'and what shadows we pursue.' Their careers are brief; their aims are cramped by their own party; their achievements are broken by their adversaries or flung aside and forgotten by posterity. If we desire to understand the forces at work around us, moulded as they are by the 'unwritten and unshaken' laws of the great Ruler of the universe, and to learn what to be prepared for in the future, it is foolish to neglect the prophetic voices, the nearer as well as the more remote.

The hundred years from the middle of the nineteenth century to the middle of the twentieth, from Lidgett's birth to his death, began roughly with the Great Exhibition of 1851, and ended with the attainment of the Welfare State and the Atom Bomb. The Great Exhibition is often said, by those who love clear-cut and rapid assertions, to have marked the peak of Victorian complacency. Queen Victoria had only been on the throne for fourteen years; but in those years the wide-spread dissatisfaction—republicanism even—that marked the time of her accession had passed away; the ominous threats of Chartism had grown silent; and the revolutionary movement which had shaken every throne in Europe had left the British monarchy stronger than before. Trade was advancing, even booming; and in every sea the guns of the British navy were feared.

Yet deep misgivings were everywhere. Carlyle and Dickens were speaking in more penetrating tones than the prophets of smooth things could utter. Shaftesbury and his growing band of followers forced reluctant eyes to behold horrors equal to those of the worst days of the Industrial Revolution. More dangerous, in the minds of many, was the shaking of foundations in the world of thought. Rome was raising her threatening head. Science, delving in the rocks, was undermining the simple truths of the Bible. Matthew Arnold was typical of many mid-Victorians, troubled as he was, and as they were, by the 'strange disease of modern life, with its sick hurry, its divided aims'. As the years went on, people were beginning to ask whether the duty of the State, no longer confined to keeping the ring and providing a fair field for each individual without favour and without injustice or illegal interference, might not be to establish and secure a decent minimum standard of life for all. Religion itself, in a society which was being driven to consider the condition of England, and the betterment of 'the labouring poor', was discovering new and disturbing influences in the Gospel, which came, as had been said, not to bring peace, but a sword.

The century through which Lidgett lived saw the gradual

spread of the new doctrine of responsibility for the non-privileged. The abolition of the slave trade, and then of slavery, has been hailed as the first great announcement of the doctrine. The far-reaching reforms which were carried through in the decade before Queen Victoria came to the throne were a reaffirmation of it. But the idea of responsibility was strictly limited and but partially understood. The satisfaction of conferring a benefit went hand in hand with the dread of facing a growing danger. If any generalization can be permitted, it is that from 1850, very slowly at first, but gaining strength steadily, a new stream of conviction was flowing: the conviction that to open the prison doors and to loose the chains of the captive, to share what we value with those to whom both nature and society have denied it, is something that we owe, not to ourselves only, but to them. It is this which has given us whatever we have to be proud of, alike in the home and the foreign policy of this country.

It is not too much to claim that Lidgett stood among the select number of those who have seen this clearly, and among the still smaller number of those who have understood it, as a demand, not simply of nature or of some innate or instinctive moral idea, but of the will and the very being of the Father of mankind.

Before fifty years of Lidgett's century were passed, we were clear that we must 'educate our masters'—up to a point, of course—and we had actually even been told that 'we are all socialists now'. But even then we were far from prepared for the vast changes we have seen in the last fifty years. Two waves of social reform have swept over us, one before the first World War, the other after the second. The duty of the State has come increasingly to be interpreted as that of providing for the wants, not only of the poor, or even of the 'deserving poor', but of all its citizens; while on the other hand, the modern attitude to religion has recalled the verdict of Bishop Butler, two hundred years earlier, that the Christian faith was falling into general disrepute. The task left to Almighty God Himself has come to be thought of as that of setting an example of general benevolence.

Such a conception of God has never aroused the emotions of His creatures. And there has been much, too, to squeeze Him out of their thoughts. The discoveries and inventions of the twentieth century (we can hardly draw the line between the two), and its social and political achievements, have brought the wonders of the physical world, unknown before even in the palace, to every cottage door; the horrors of sweated labour have been replaced by the enjoyments of leisure; distances almost unchanged since the days of the Romans have been all but annihilated; and we are now on the brink of becoming the agents of new powers which seem likely either to transform human life or to destroy it. We may well be forgiven for asking, in a period of such bewildering 'progress', to what new Niagara we are hurrying.

To such a question neither this book nor any other can give an answer. But no thoughtful student either of the past or the present can ignore or neglect it. And these chapters, dealing with the career of one who touched the life of the whole period with no uncertain hand cannot but be of value to those who inherit the hopes as well as the fears of preceding generations. History, we are assured, never repeats itself. We are all thankful to know that. But just as, so they say, there are only twelve stories, with their variants, that have ever been told, so, we may perhaps add, there are no more than twelve questions that can be asked. They are asked, like the riddle of the Sphinx, in different words; but to see how wise men have dealt with the problems of their day has more than a biographical interest for us who have to deal with the problems of our own.

This book makes no attempt to offer a biography of Dr Lidgett. It is its aim to give what could not be looked for from a biography. It endeavours to show the importance he attached to the questions of his time, the fashion of his approach to them, the nature of his aims, and the extent of his influence. The chapter which is allotted to me is occupied chiefly with a single section of the earlier part of his life, not so much because of any special interest that those years might arouse, but because, at least to those who knew him somewhat intimately at that time, the leading motifs, as they might be called, were then given out, one after another, and familiarity with them as they were then to be heard may assist the reader to appreciate the fuller orchestration of succeeding years.

To many people, Dr Lidgett's name is still most closely associated with the Bermondsey Settlement. He had been fifteen years in the Ministry when he went to live for the rest of his life in Bermondsey. At the time he was little known outside the circuits in which, as Methodists say, he had 'travelled'. Once the Settlement was started, it was not long before he was widely known as its Warden, even by many who would never have given a thought to the simple Methodist minister. Even in those first years he began to make his mark in public and administrative life, as well as in the concerns of the Methodist Church as a whole. His theological writing, too, was begun as soon as he was fixed in the Settlement. In a few years he was able to give considerable time to the organization of education, a subject in which he took hereditary and ever-deepening interest; and throughout the years which followed he was looked to as the leader of the progressive elements in the London County Council, which commenced its career two years before he came to Bermondsey, and, in other circles, as the centre of all that made for closer co-operation and (a hope that lay near to his heart) union between the Churches.

To the Settlement then let us turn, as he saw it and moulded it, and as others came to it, in its earlier days. But to understand it as he saw it (and this is to understand him), we must look at the thirty-one years through which, as he himself was firmly convinced, he was being guided to Bermondsey. He was born in what would be called a 'good' Methodist family, pious, prosperous, with a flourishing business in the city and a comfortable suburban house at Blackheath, a family keenly and generously interested in all that could be called Methodist, one in which all its members knew their Bible and their Hymnbook, attended the means of grace regularly, and were expected to take an active part in the work of their chapel. They resented being spoken of as 'Dissenters'; they feared any intrusion of what could be called politics into the life of their Church; they were kind to their inferiors, but acutely conscious of social barriers not to be crossed; sympathetic to their workpeople, but resolved to tolerate no interference with the conduct of their business or their factories.

For a lad born in such surroundings, a commercial career seemed the natural opening. He had imagined himself at one time as a barrister; but the young John Scott was by nature a student and a voracious reader, with a talent for reading the right books. His memory was remarkably retentive; his mind was in the best sense critical, quick to discern between the genuine and the pretentious; and he wrote with a speed and a precision that many a professional literary man would envy. He made his way at once to the heart of every subject, as of every situation in which he found himself, and like Wordsworth's Happy Warrior, he came to see what he foresaw. Had he entered one of the older Universities, and there perhaps joined the Established Church, the highest posts might have been open to him. But he was never known to express regret that he had matriculated at the University of London, which later on was to receive, and requite, great and continuous services from him.

As a student, he seemed marked out for a theologian; and it was his good fortune, or something more, while moving in circles where a good deal of arid theology was being written and preached, to come under the notice and influence of Dr W. B. Pope, who among Methodist theological writers displayed, like his friend Dr W. F. Moulton, the 'gentleness of wisdom'. While at London University he became conscious of a definite call to the Wesleyan Ministry. His parents, after some hesitation, acquiesced; and without any period of training at a theological seminary, he found himself, as a circuit minister, in a vigorous industrial town—an entire change from his home at Blackheath—in Northern Staffordshire. The Wesleyan system then meant moving to a new sphere every three years; and his next period of ministerial life, after Tunstall, was passed at Southport, almost a kind of Blackheath over again; then Cardiff, a complete contrast, where coal and iron were turning a small town into a huge city, with all the extremes produced by a frenzy of industrialism. Then he went on to Wolverhampton, where he found similar conditions: even when employers and employed were linked by a common religious and denominational interest, they were happier when worshipping in different sanctuaries. He knew a further contrast on his removal to Cambridge.

Another man might have said: 'Study is my true *métier*; and here at Cambridge I can at last carry it out.' It would have been easy to do so. The University was hospitable to Methodism. Dr Moulton, one of the revisers of the New Testament, whose work had appeared nine years before, was the Head of The Leys School, only recently founded, but already making its name; from him young Lidgett received every encouragement. Moreover, it was one of Lidgett's duties to come into touch with the Methodist undergraduates, and to this congenial task he gave himself at once.

But after the varied experiences of the past twelve years, he had taken with him to Cambridge a deep impression of the social and industrial as well as the religious needs of the country. He had seen wealth and poverty dwelling side by side, and yet with an enduring and seemingly impassable gulf between them. He had known the brave but sadly limited attempts of organized Church life to bridge it. And now he found himself where there was talk about a bridge of a new kind. Cambridge had an effect on him which must have surprised many of his friends. It made him less rather than more academic, or rather, it turned the tide of his academic interest into the channel of what was then called social reform, but which was in reality, for him, something far larger. He attributed his conviction that he was intended to offer for the Ministry to a sermon which he had heard as a lad; and he loved to recall how, some months after his arrival in Cambridge, while walking back one November evening from a village service, he solemnly devoted himself to give practical and permanent effect to the feeling which a sermon of his own had already provoked, by 'planting a colony' in one of the poorest districts of London, a colony 'evangelical, but with the broadest possible educational and social aims'. Mrs S. A. Barnett tells how a similar moment of dedication came to her husband and herself on a Sunday morning at Mentone, before the first definite step was taken toward the founding of Toynbee Hall.

Such was the birth of the project of the Bermondsey Settlement. The Settlement idea, as we may call it, was not new. It had three roots. The first could be found in Ferdinand Lassalle's words, written in the sixties: 'Man has been released successively from a state of legal dependence and one of intellectual dependence; he must now be released from one of economic dependence.' Fifty years after, Benjamin Kidd wrote: 'The political enfranchisement of the masses is nearly accomplished; the process which will occupy the next period will be that of their social enfranchisement.'

The second was the sense of disturbance, widespread, but often unnoticed by those who did not actually share the miseries beneath the surface of Victorian prosperity. Pharisees and Levites, lay and clerical, of all professions and callings, passed by on the other side. Carlyle and Ruskin had thundered against the heartlessness which tolerated these miseries; Maurice and the Christian Socialists lifted quieter but not less searching voices. Maurice's Working-men's College had been founded in 1854. J. S. Mill, who had expressed in his book *On Liberty* his fears that the provision of State machinery would dwarf the individual, was moving toward his later and more human standpoint, that the doctrine of *laissez faire* (the State as merely the ring-master) was tyranny to the unprivileged, and that 'the State cannot afford pauperism any more than slavery'. Karl Marx had been working day after day at the British Museum Library with his blood on fire at the distresses of the proletariat. The sober English public was startled and angered by Hyndman and Blatchford. It was frightened by the great depression of 1878-9, and by publications like *How the Poor Live* and Preston's *Bitter Cry of Darkest London* (1883). 'Here we see', men said, 'what our fathers read about as the "Two Nations". Are they still to be two?'

The third root was a feeling which by its very nature would appeal to relatively few. Faced by such revelations as these, the ordinary Englishman is wont to demand fresh legislation or some new institution, or a charitable society; the more adventurous spirits will form a union like the Social Democratic Federation (1882) or the milder Fabian Society (1884). But another attitude was possible: to go down to those dreary dwellings and see, and act, for oneself. It was gradually to become clear that, as Lidgett wrote in 1906, 'the key to all social questions is to be found in spiritual and not in merely material conditions'. It was characteristic of him as a biblical expositor that he turned more often to the Fourth Gospel than to the other three. In such a way of thinking, the first step toward any improvement is the birth of the friendship that rises from personal knowledge.

Was the gulf between the 'two nations' unbridgeable? The administration of the Poor Law, both before and after 1834, seemed worse than useless; but sporadic attempts had long been made toward befriending the friendless. The Stranger's Friend Society (1785), The Society for Improving the Condition of the Labouring Classes (1844), The Society for the Relief of Distress (1860), and the Charity Organization Society (1869), had all done their best. But there were the 'poor' still, speaking a different language, recognizing different standards of life and behaviour, living in a different world, and yet, geographically, how close! Cross a street or two, and you were in their midst. True, topography by itself has little to do with the matter. There is no place where one can so easily and fatally jostle a man's body and yet be miles away from him in spirit, as in the mean streets of London. Yet physical proximity is the beginning. Neighbourhood can lead to neighbourliness as nothing else can. Spending a night in a casual ward or twenty-four hours in a condemned tenement can teach more than a score of books or reports. If one cannot actually bear the sorrows of the poor, he can at least experience the frustrations of their lives. This had been attempted by Edward Denison, who at the age of twenty-seven came to London to live among the poor. He had met John Richard Green and Brook Lambert in 1869 to discuss the possibilities of 'doing something for the poor', and was giving religious instruction to working men in

1870. But few people with responsibilities of their own could follow Edward Denison into the slums.

What could be seriously suggested was that educated people might be brought to live among the poor in University Settlements, 'communities of men and women associated to spread knowledge'. 'Bad habits in rich and poor may be cured by contact.' Such were the arguments urged in Oxford Common Rooms by a young London clergyman, S. A. Barnett. The memorandum of a Cambridge Settlement looked to 'an association of persons with different opinions and different tastes; its methods are spiritual; it aims at permeation rather than conversion; its trust is in friends.'

Such men and women, it was urged, whether in lodgings or in Settlements, live their own lives, without asceticism or superiority, learning as much as teaching, receiving as much as giving. 'Culture spreads by contact.' 'It is distance', as Barnett told the undergraduates in 1883, 'that makes friendship between classes almost impossible; and therefore residence among the poor is suggested as a simple way in which University men may serve their generation. By sharing their fuller lives and riper thoughts with the poor, they will destroy the root evil of poverty.'

This naïve faith in the value of simple contact with 'the poor' (how often the unhappy phrase meets us!) was liable to some rude shocks; but without such contact what other starting-point could be found? At all events, it led to the discovery of the positive dangers of charity, the misbegotten child of ignorance and indolence. Better than indiscriminate giving, people began to reflect, were the relentless investigations and tabulations of the London Charity Organization Society, to whom, its enemies said, the formulation of a need was far more important than its conquest. Charity had been a virtue; it was becoming a profession. Taught by such hard lessons as the successive waves of distress and the failures of Mansion House Relief Funds, the public came to see that nothing is more difficult than effective giving, that helping the destitute is a fine art, and that sharing, the only way in which spiritual values can be imparted, means mutual knowledge. 'Morality', as Arnold Toynbee had said, 'must be linked with economics as a practical science.'

These were the pleas urged by one who might well be called the father of Settlements, S. A. Barnett. An Oxford man, without the record of a specially distinguished career at his University, he had the good sense to keep up his University friendships, and the happiness, later, to marry a woman as eager and devoted as himself. After six years as a curate at St Mary's, Bryanstone Square, he became, in 1873, at the age of twenty-nine, the vicar of one of the worst parishes in East London. Preaching was useless; charity was worse than useless. He and his wife could only see one door of hope. If a number of men of culture and ideals would come down into this forlorn region and by sheer force of personal influence and faith lift its victims into the light of decency and good behaviour, the Kingdom of Heaven would be served at last.

For some ten years the Barnetts paid visits to Oxford, and gradually fired both dons and undergraduates by their vision. The great Jowett, who advised his students to 'make some friendships with the poor', arranged meeting after meeting for them in Balliol, until at last the project began to take shape. An old house was acquired and reconstructed in Whitechapel; a large sum of money was raised from both Universities; and in 1884, eleven years after Barnett had first gone to the East End, the Hall was opened, to accommodate, besides the Warden and his wife, fourteen residents. These included Lyttelton Gell, Bolton King, and Hancock Nunn. The Hall was named after Arnold Toynbee, whose book, *The Industrial Revolution*, might have served as a preparatory work for all intending residents, and who, unhappily, died just before the Hall began its career.

Three other Settlements followed rapidly: Oxford House (1884), which was as anxious to maintain a close connexion with the Anglican Church as Toynbee was to avoid it; Caius House (1887), founded by Gonville and Caius College, Cambridge; and Mansfield House (1890), linked with the Congregational Mansfield College at Oxford. Mansfield House started the provision of a Poor Man's Lawyer, now widely taken up; but it subsequently ceased to receive residents. In 1934 the number of residential Settlements had grown to twenty-nine in London, and to fifteen elsewhere in the country. Hull House, Chicago, was opened as a Women's University Settlement by Miss Jane Addams, one of the ablest of America's splendid band of women social servants. In 1892, in a dingy back street in Bermondsey, the Bermondsey Settlement was opened; and to that Settlement we must now return.

Like Toynbee Hall, the Bermondsey Settlement, humanly speaking, would never have been opened, save for the faith and resolution of one man. Barnett, however, had some of the most influential people in Oxford and outside behind him, and could draw on the large resources of wealthy and generous Anglicans. Lidgett had formed no connexions at all with Oxford, and but few, in the short time he had been resident there, with Cambridge. Without the help of Dr Moulton, to whom reference has already been made, himself not a Cambridge man, but the object there of universal respect as a scholar and a Christian, Lidgett could hardly have taken his first step.

Further, while Barnett could arrange to be more or less free to go up and down the country, Lidgett was tied to the work of his Church in Cambridge; and when, in spite of these difficulties, the time for organization and planning had come, the Wesleyan system made it necessary that the whole scheme should be laid before the annual Conference of the Church. Barnett could do almost what he liked if his Bishop did not choose to oppose him. Lidgett had to gain official approval for every step he took. He might have the support of a few prominent persons; but if he had not been able, to some extent at least, to carry with him the general body of opinion among ministers and laymen, the Settlement project would have been impossible.

And yet to gain this approval was in those days no easy matter. Wesleyans had then a very strong and on the whole salutary, though sometimes exaggerated, fear of 'politics in the pulpit'. They had an equally strong fear of any preaching that could not be called evangelical. Services, groups for edification and Bible study, meetings to support missions at home and abroad or to advocate temperance, as well as bazaars and other means of raising money, were naturally encouraged. But an institution, carried on under the auspices of the Church, which should arrange secular lectures and classes, games, clubs, concerts, and physical training, and where Church monies were not to be raised but spent, was regarded as a different matter. The Wesleyan judgement was certainly stricter than the Anglican or Congregational was likely to be; and it could be more effectively enforced.

But at last the obstacles were cleared away. The Wesleyan Conference of 1891, over which Dr Moulton presided, gave its official permission; the necessary funds were raised, from Methodists, from local sympathizers, and from a few more distant sources; and in January 1892 the main building was opened. It was to be the Warden's home for fifty-nine years. The building was grim and the surroundings were sordid; but for him at least it was lit up by faith, hope, and an undying love.

Lidgett was well aware of the strength of the opposition; but he was the last man to allow himself to be influenced by it. He knew that any pronouncements he made would be closely and even severely scrutinized. But he had made up his mind; and at the outset he defined his aims for the Settlement under six heads, as follows:

(1) To bring additional force and attractiveness to Christian work;

(2) To become a centre of social life, where all classes may meet together on equal terms for healthful intercourse and recreation;

(3) To give facilities for the study of literature, history, science, and art;

(4) To bring men together; to discuss general and special social evils and to seek their remedy;

(5) To take such part in local administration and philanthropy as may be possible;

(6) And so to do all this that it shall be perfectly clear that no mere sectarian advantage is sought, but that it shall be possible for all good men to associate themselves with our work.

If some within his own Church were likely to frown on one or another of these sentences, he was sure of sympathy from outside. But his loyalty to his convictions and his position as a Wesleyan minister, if it did not overcome all the suspicions of his fellow-Methodists, was a little puzzling to the leaders of the Settlement movement as a whole. With his social and educational aims, all the Settlements then in existence would heartily agree. Toynbee Hall would have extended the social and quasi-secular designs; Oxford House the religious, and would have urged the necessity of a stricter conformity to ecclesiastical demands; Mansfield House, perhaps, would have amplified the reference to political and municipal activities. One duty, however, descended on the Warden of the Bermondsey Settlement himself from which the other heads of Settlements were free, but which he had no idea of neglecting. He was the superintendent of the Wesleyan circuit in Bermondsey; that is, he was responsible for the oversight of the work of four places of worship; and he was expected ordinarily to conduct two services every Sunday, to preside over all official meetings of the circuit, and to guide its religious life.

To most men these duties would have made up a full-time occupation. Those who watched Lidgett in the early years in Bermondsey saw him, in addition, superintending every detail of the day-to-day life of the Settlement household, planning lectures, courses of study, recreational clubs and societies, and finding leaders for all kinds of movements, literary, social, musical, and religious, which already existed or might be brought into existence in those dreary streets. They saw a kind of second Settlement, a Women's House, taking shape about a mile away, with a director who revealed, like the Warden himself, a surprising combination of level-headedness and impetuosity, and whose residents, unlike their male and slightly contemptuous opposite numbers in the men's settlement at Farncombe Street, gave their whole time to the duties assigned to them.

No one could enter into any sort of intimacy with the Warden in those early days—an intimacy which, in spite of a certain ingrained shyness, he was almost pathetically anxious to gain—

without being aware of the feelers for friendship and understanding which he was continually putting out. He was alert from the beginning to detect every opportunity for swinging into the ampler tides of industrial and political life which flowed round the Settlement. Here he could hardly expect his small body of residents to follow him. Of these young men more will be said later; but while his knowledge of local conditions and needs, as time went on, left most of them behind, he would surprise them by the expression of a view on a philosophical or religious subject which would remind some of them of things they had heard in University circles or college discussions by Cam or Isis, but which were strange to the sights and smells of the Surrey Commercial Docks. The result was that they hardly knew whether to be more astonished that a Methodist minister could talk now like a labour leader and now like a don, or that one who might have been a labour leader or a don could be a Methodist minister, or that, with his wide outlook and his exalted ambitions, he was content to make his home in Bermondsey. They would perhaps have been more surprised to learn that, outlasting all his colleagues in the movement, he was to remain the head of his Settlement as well as the Superintendent of his circuit through all the long years of his active life.

Why did Lidgett choose the South of London for his Settlement when the attention of the public was turned to the East End and its bitter cry? The answer can be given in his own words: because Bermondsey was 'at that time the most neglected neighbourhood of poorer London, as far as the purposes I had in contemplation were concerned'. The 'South Side' was practically off the map, derelict. It had neither the advantages nor the disadvantages of the appalling East End. It had not been written up like the Mile End Road or the Ratcliffe Highway. It offered no field for slumming by society women. There was nothing picturesque or romantic about its monotonous poverty. No one had ever gone there to gain the benefit of making friends with the poor. 'It appeared', said Charles Booth, 'to lack independent life.'

Yet in its squalid way it could provide plenty of material for such a search. It contained acres and acres of docks; and docks then meant chronic unemployment, the neighbour both of exasperation and despair. It found room for few large factories, but for much casual labour. Spacious dwellings, once luxurious and ornate, had fallen into a decay as hopeless as that of the alleys and courts which crowded round them. Labour was apathetic; hopes and ideals had been driven out by petty intrigues and personal quarrels. A few churches, rising, like the public houses, above the sea of chimney-pots visible from the railway train, claimed to be 'holding their own'. But their congregations, clinging desperately to their respectability, knew as little of their neighbours as did the exalted dwellers in Streatham and Dulwich; and their well-meant attempts at charity, the only kind of service open to them or conceivable by them, simply roused the cringing resentment of their victims, and the scorn and horror of charity organization societies.

The Dock strike of 1889 had brought undoubted benefits to the South as to the North side of the river; but it had seemed to heighten the contrast between those who were above and those who were still below the poverty line. It would be absurd to suppose that all who were beneath that line were vicious or degraded; but there was nothing to break the drab and, in the dark courts, the filthy monotony of life and outlook, save the gaunt and forbidding Board Schools whose influence strove in vain to lift up what the home was constantly dragging down. It was to such a region as this that Lidgett decided to apply Barnett's 'Let us know, and know the worst'.

Lidgett, however, did not go, or ask others to go, to Bermondsey simply to learn the worst. He was taking what he felt for that region to be the best. Plenty of people would have understood and might have supported an evangelistic 'mission'. But it was more than a mission in that sense which he had in mind. 'A settlement', he wrote, 'is or should be a community of social workers who come to a poor neighbourhood to assist by the methods of friendship and co-operation in building all that is essential to the well-being of the neighbourhood.' Hence, freedom and initiative are of its essence. . . . A cut-and-dried programme would be fatal both to the conception and to the development of a Settlement. Its head should not stereotype, but guide and co-ordinate all its activities, encouraging adventure, but tempering it with prudence. Much therefore will depend on the temperament and outlook of the settlers who rally to his banner. Hence, for more than the ordinary reasons, there must be a considerable interval between the ideal and the practicable. The Settlement was to be a little University, teaching the *omne scibile*, whatever could be known: a community of capable cultured men, teaching, studying, playing, praying together. And it gave him the experience and the opportunities that he hoped it would give to all its members.

'Tempering it with prudence'—that was characteristic of the young Warden. But the programme fell none the less strangely on Methodist ears. And there were few besides Methodists to whom the Warden, before all things a Methodist minister, could appeal, either for money, for sympathy, or for recruits. The generosity of Methodism was ample; but its field was narrow. The building of schools and hospitals on the Mission Field was not then above suspicion. To preach the Gospel, the paramount duty of the Church of Christ, meant for most Methodists to aim directly at the conversion of individuals. But the Manchester Mission, started in 1886 by S. F. Collier, followed in a year by the West London Mission under the innovating guidance of Hugh Price Hughes, was forcing its supporters to recognize the connexion between the needs of the body and of the spirit. The same period saw the rise of the romantic work of the East London Mission of Peter Thompson, close to Toynbee Hall; and the Home provided by T. B. Stephenson, the Methodist, as those of Dr Barnardo, for the 'poor little perishing souls' who filled the streets of the city, exercised an irresistible appeal. But the suspicion was there, and behind the suspicion was the fear of a sudden call for political action and the too drastic response that might follow.

There were eager Liberals and no less eager though less numerous Conservatives, who applauded each step in this 'forward movement'; but when at the inaugural meeting of the

West London Mission an allusion to Mr Gladstone roused a burst of applause, it was not only the Conservatives who shook grave and critical heads. Others, not a few, asked: 'What is Methodism going to get out of it?' Bermondsey, on the other hand, wondered what this Settlement was up to; what was its game? Was it a new dodge of the Churches—we had not then learnt to talk about dopes and opiates—or of the rich, or of a political party, or was it another attack on the pleasures of the poor? It seemed little likely to put more money into empty pockets. It was an irruption of intruders, speaking a strange language. Why could they not leave other people alone? In the nineties, too, labour was becoming more independent, and less anxious for help from a middle-class movement like a Settlement.

Such criticisms, both local and ecclesiastical, not seldom vigorously outspoken, could only be met by courage, faith, and a profound sense of vocation. But they were met; and into those gloomy surroundings, so different from his preceding circuits, and those in which he might have expected to travel, Lidgett brought his family as into his promised land.

It was no small thing which, in doing this, he asked of his wife. The doors into ever-widening fields of work which from the first opened to him were doors through which in the nature of things she could not pass. But she bravely and resolutely took her part in the work of the Settlement; and, when, forty-four years after the Settlement opened, she passed to her reward, her husband was conscious of a loneliness he had never been allowed to feel before.

The tall building, rising from an asphalt yard in its back street, had little form or comeliness to recommend it on the outside. But it had been suitably planned within. A large hall for lectures and concerts, a gymnasium and games-room, class-rooms of various sizes, and a library, somewhat sparsely furnished, welcomed the intending students; a dining-hall, a series of bed-sitting rooms for the residents, a common-room and the Warden's flat were all to be found upstairs; while, in quarters of their own, were established a most capable and devoted caretaker and his wife.

In the residents there could hardly be expected that sense of dedication and self-sacrifice which they came to see in the Warden. For most of them, working in offices in London during the day, the Settlement offered a convenient and not unpleasant lodging. Unlike the residents in Toynbee Hall and Oxford House, few of them at first were University men.

In spite of all the education that preceded and followed the inauguration of Toynbee Hall, the general level of opinion on social matters in Oxford was primitive. There was quite an excitement in one College, for instance, in the early nineties, when it was discovered that 'a real live Socialist' had been entertained for the week-end. At another, an innocent meeting of the Wesley Society was humorously mobbed 'because', complained the undergraduates, 'there was a Socialist meeting in the college last week, and we are going to have no more of that sort of thing'. Charles Gore, subsequently Bishop of Oxford, and one of the few dons at that time who cared for the souls of undergraduates, and who moreover called himself a Socialist, inspired a small company—were they to be considered the descendants of Ruskin's band of road-makers?—to hunt up Socialistic passages in the Church Fathers, though, because of the lack of either material or of interest, their labours soon came to an end.

It may have been therefore of little disadvantage to the Settlement that the proportion of University men among the residents was not high. But a rather large number of these looked forward to spending no more than two or three years there. All were, however, expected to give some help and leadership in their spare time to Settlement concerns; and this was not hard for young Methodists who were accustomed to sing 'A charge to keep I have'.

Their personal relations with the Warden varied. All met at dinner; but the Warden's shyness was something of a barrier, and in his desire to explain his view of a speech or a public event, he was apt at times to forget his duties as carver of the joint for which a tableful of hungry men was waiting. Some of the younger residents were naturally in awe of him, though of most of them he would ask at times, in genuine humility:

'Did you approve of this?' or 'Did I say the right thing about that?' He did not talk as if he were addressing a public meeting or preaching to a congregation; yet there was always something, even in his table-talk, which smacked of the lecture-room. You had the impression that his ideas on every subject were astonishingly well-drilled. You would not perhaps imagine how he could have got them to the parade ground; but they would always come forward at the word of command. He could be witty, incisive, even at times pungent. 'Ah, your rich men! Smoke their cigars, but don't let them lead you by the nose.' On the other hand, his sentences, though naturally more often in the pulpit than on the platform, would reach a portentous length. In later years, a President of the Methodist Conference remarked from the chair with a smile how often Dr Lidgett's periods recalled the first chapter of the Epistle to the Ephesians. There were some, however, who were not in awe of him: notably W. E. Brunyate, second wrangler and a fellow of Trinity College, Cambridge, who was later to become the adviser to the Khedive's Government in Cairo. He was of great assistance to the Warden in more ways than one (he came into residence in 1893); but he made it his business to pour cold water on the whole affair—we were never quite sure how much was in jest—and to assure the younger men that the Settlement was doomed to failure. This was in complete contrast to Dr C. W. Kimmins, also of Cambridge, who came to the Settlement soon after. He was, later, the chief inspector of education to the London County Council, and, as a psychologist, he specialized in the laughter of children. Nothing gave him greater pleasure than to play the laughing philosopher to the Heraclitean reflections of his friend. Another Cambridge man was R. V. N. Hopkins, who, as Sir Richard Hopkins, K.C.B., became the head of Somerset House and of the Treasury. None of the residents was better loved in Bermondsey than Dr Alfred Salter, M.P. for Bermondsey for some years. The Settlement Sick Insurance Society, which he founded in 1910, numbered nine thousand members in 1947. His wife, who had been a resident at the Women's House, became the Mayor of Bermondsey.

To most of the residents the work of the Settlement was only a part-time occupation. None of them had the benefit of any previous training in social work or observation, nor in those earlier days was such training considered necessary. Both Warden and residents had to feel their way to the tasks that called for them. But there was plenty of good-will; and if the average resident did not play his part with conspicuous success, the wonder is that he played it at all. Lectures on all kinds of subjects were provided, and classes were formed in languages, mathematics, public health, and even theology. One of the residents found himself helping a small Jewish boy with his Hebrew.[1] Coaching for examinations, and running clubs, entertainments, concerts, and parties of all kinds, helped the young residents to the discovery of themselves. The University Extension Movement was already on its feet, but its lectures were not intended for such audiences as Bermondsey or Whitechapel could provide. Yet the lectures quietly arranged by the residents were prophetic of the Workers' Educational Association. A rather disreputable public house was converted into the St George's Club for men in 1895 and opened with 162 members. In 1897 Lidgett was elected, along with Miss Honor Morton, a Woman Resident, to the London School Board, and in 1905 he became an Alderman of the London County Council, and remained one of its leading members till his retirement in 1928.

One of the early residents, John Borland, later the musical adviser to the Educational Committee of the LCC, found at the Settlement the opportunity not only for a strikingly successful choral society, but for continual inspiration to music-lovers in South London; nor will his contemporaries at the Settlement forget his informal Sunday evening piano recitals when the day's work was done.

Criticisms were heard, as we have noticed, that the Settlement was not sufficiently religious. But religion means more than the holding of services and meetings on Church premises. No one could live near the Settlement in Bermondsey or

[1] This was the author of this chapter, who has modestly concealed the fact that he was an early resident in the Settlement—ED.

Rotherhithe without deploring the presence of wild young lads on the streets; this was in days before we began to hear about gangs and juvenile delinquency. The Warden approached one of his residents, a diffident bank clerk, and a great admirer of Henry George, to form a Boys' Brigade. The young clerk was sure that he was not meant for such a piece of work, and most of his friends agreed with him. But the Warden persisted—he knew his man—and in a year or two, the newly formed company, quarried out of the roughest material, numbered more than a hundred lads, as keen as their officers, and the Sunday Bible-class was the best attended and most orderly gathering of the week. It is now one of the best companies in London. Mr Rippon, the first captain, whose simple secret was personal devotion to the needs of each of his boys, was succeeded in the command by two other residents, one of whom is now Major Norman Lewis, D.S.O.

Perhaps the chief significance of the Settlement is that for the sixty years of its existence it has served as a centre or 'jumping-off place' for the activities of workers of all kinds who would never have found their way to Bermondsey without the Settlement and its Warden, and would never have functioned save on such fallow ground as was waiting at Bermondsey to be dug up. Sometimes it was the teasing persistence of the gad-fly which was felt; sometimes the beneficent operation of the intellectual or spiritual midwife; or co-operation with local officials who had the faith and the hope, but not, unhappily, the initiative. It might be the humble task of canvassing or distributing bills, or supporting a progressive candidate at a meeting, that set a young man on the path of service; it might be the running of a branch of the children's Country Holiday Fund (a highly educational piece of work), or, at the Women's House, of the Metropolitan Association for Befriending Young Servants (how odd this sounds today). One of the subsidiary results, as they might be called, of the presence in Bermondsey of the Settlement and its Warden was the Beatrice Club for women and girls, whose aim was 'to help those who have but little opportunity for reaching even the fringe of all that is good in life to something of what ought to be theirs by right of citizenship'.

It had its origin in Dr Lidgett's chairmanship of the Rotherhithe Infirmary, in the desire of a life-long sufferer whom Dr Lidgett had known in his Cambridge days to be of some use to others who were as limited as herself, and in the initiative of a girl employed at Peek Frean's Bermondsey factory who brought a hundred of her fellow-workers to the Club's first meeting.

A more spectacular example is the starting of the work for cripples, carried out at 'the public school of crippledom', the Heritage craft schools. It developed from the Guild of the Brave Poor Things, transferred soon after its birth in 1894 from the West London Mission to the Settlement. The Warden of the Settlement watched over its early steps till its removal in 1903 to Chailey, and was for forty years the Chairman of the Governors. Lidgett's long experience, ready sympathy, and wide aquaintance with people of influence and position made him of invaluable assistance to projects of all kinds. Thus in 1898 he organized a series of picture exhibitions in St George's House; in 1927 he purchased a country home near Leith Hill for the use of LCC school-children and others; and in his later years, when he was giving up much of his public work, he interested himself in a private venture for dealing with problem children which combined scientific principles and Christian devotion; the public support which he could secure and, not less valuable, his own encouragement and advice, turned anxiety into confidence and success. Men in all walks of life, who have not been in South London for years, will confess that their abiding sense of obligation to share what they most value with others—an obligation which surely lies at the heart of religion—was born in the mean streets of Bermondsey. *C'est le premier pas qui coûte.*

The last few paragraphs will have shown the extent to which the Warden *was* the Settlement. Without the winning charm of Canon Barnett and his wife, and equally without the officer-like precision felt in the first head of Oxford House, Lidgett made and left his mark everywhere. He did not unbutton his heart; he seldom showed, even in his more intimate moments, his deep natural affections. There were times in his study when he and his most trusted allies would raise their voices in heated altercation, to the embarrassment of the casual bystander; yet no one could fail to recognize his selfless dedication to what was, for him, the manifestation of the glory of God.

But there was one gift which many found and remembered in him more clearly than in anyone else they had known. It was itself a compound of several qualities not often observed together. In the first place, until the last years, he never seemed to know weariness as most men know it, and this tirelessness was joined to a zest for individual contacts. In the anxious months of the first World War he would return to the Settlement at ten o'clock after one or more exhausting meetings, to find forty or fifty letters prepared by his secretary for his inspection and signature. He would scan each one critically, and then ask for details about his students, of most of whom he seemed to have personal knowledge. Secondly, a capacity for making each person whom he met feel 'I am the centre of his interest', was joined to a rare social sense and unerring tact, and led him beneath the surface in dealing with all sorts and conditions of men and women, giving him an almost uncanny skill in managing them. He would never drive; he could always lead; and even those who least understood the nature of his influence over them felt for him a mixture of respect and affection which was born of the real affection, often unsuspected, and seldom if ever expressed, which he felt for them.

The above reflections are necessary for an estimate of any part of Lidgett's activity. His life was throughout a remarkable instance of integration. Like Arnold's Scholar-gypsy, he had 'one aim, one purpose, one desire'; and in spite of the disappointments and rebuffs that are the lot of all leaders of men, he was content to wait for the star from heaven to fall.

Unlike the first Warden of Toynbee, he never contemplated removal. The most he allowed himself and his family was the weekly afternoon at his old home in Blackheath, and the annual holiday in the country. Even then a case of books and papers and reports would accompany him, to the dismay of his children. Forty years on, when nearly all his old supporters were no more, when his wife had been called from his side, and the German bombs were threatening to bring all his ideals crashing to the ground, he was found seated alone in a little room—one of the few undamaged by recent raids—with his books round him, bowed by the weight of nearly ninety years, yet vigorous in spirit as ever and making fresh plans for the future.

By that time, the critical voices, so persistent in his earlier years, had died down. In Methodism, and outside, he was a venerable yet still youthful link with the disappearing past, though the deeper springs of action in his prolonged life were but half understood by his contemporaries and their successors. For more than a generation he had imparted a certain stability to the progressives around him, the source alike of caution and encouragement. The band of impulsive young men who, in the early years of the century, had followed S. E. Keeble in the formation of the 'Methodist Union for Social Service', felt, when Lidgett joined them, something of the relief of which John Henry Newman and his fellow Tractarians were conscious when they could look on the venerated Pusey as their leader; and the motto of the Union, 'See and Serve', might have been chosen for the Settlement itself. Those who heard his speech at the inaugural meeting of the Union at City Road Chapel in 1905 will not forget the scorn he poured on its Pharisaic critics who held that to do one's duty and love one's neighbour was not 'spiritual'.

Lidgett's work for Methodist Union and on the London County Council, which was already taking up much of his interest, is dealt with at length elsewhere in this book. But this seems the place to deviate somewhat from an account of the Settlement and to refer briefly to his editorial work and to his relation with Hugh Price Hughes, who at the height of his power was the best-known religious leader in the country, and the most loved and the most dreaded man in Methodism. Born seven years before Lidgett, he was drawing the notice of all London, putting the Gospel into the news, as it were, by his Sunday afternoon Conferences at St James's Hall, while Lidgett was laying the foundation of his work in the back streets of Bermondsey. Hughes's appeal to the Nonconformist Conscience became a political war-cry, brought the career of

THE WARDEN OF THE BERMONDSEY SETTLEMENT 65

Parnell to a sudden and undignified end, and thus affected, for good or ill, the whole future of Ireland. A 'Rupert of Debate' —the title is as appropriate to Hughes as to anyone—he could sweep his audiences in directions which neither they nor he anticipated. His sword was at the service of every generous cause; and aided by the quiet courage and caution of his noble wife, he gave by his 'Forward Movement' an impulse to both Methodism and the Free Churches which they have never lost.

Lidgett had no thought of making or breaking a politician or an ecclesiastic; but he was consulted by all, and generally got what he wanted. Both men were necessary; but it was a happy thing for the Church, in its narrower and its wider interests, that Hughes came first. When Lidgett left the field, just fifty years after Hughes's career was suddenly cut short, almost all that Hughes had fought for and even despaired of had been won.

When Hughes died, Lidgett quietly took both his editorial chair in the *Methodist Times* and his place at the head of the Forward Movement, with the sure hand, not of a journalist only, but of a statesman and scholar. He brought the same qualities to the *Contemporary Review*, which, edited by Sir Percy Bunting along with G. P. Gooch, was widely known as the Liberal organ which joined sanity to adventurousness. After the death of the former in 1911, Lidgett took his place by Gooch's side. Meanwhile a stream of theological books was flowing from his pen, almost as if it had no other occupation.

In his later years he surprised his friends by his appreciation of beauty and his observation of every detail in his surroundings; and he delighted them by the unfailing gaiety and boyishness of his manner, his skill in talking to boys and girls, and his power of treating every person with whom he spoke as demanding his whole attention. He summed up the aims of his life in a remarkable address at a luncheon given in his honour in 1949; and he did not hide his happiness when, in 1952, he received the freedom of the Borough of Bermondsey. But it was highly appropriate that the last public utterance of one who was from first to last a Methodist minister should be an address on John and Charles Wesley at the Eighth Ecumenical

Methodist Conference in the University Church in Oxford.

The preceding pages have attempted to expound Lidgett's conception of the Settlement. What of the wider work to which the Settlement led him? As we have already seen, he did not begin as a social reformer or as a public man. He began with a deeply rooted sense both of the theological relation of God to man and the religious duty of embodying the responsibilities of this relation in every department of human life. He went on to found a community in which this embodiment could be carried out. Similar in its general aims to other communities or settlements founded about the same time, it was unique in its religious emphasis and its connexion with a particular denomination, combined with the championship of every good cause which it could assist. 'All social service', he would insist, 'manifests and is inspired by the fatherhood of God.' He thus found himself in a position in which his loyalty to his Church and to his place in it could be applied with a breadth and an emphasis rarely possible.

To the resulting many-sidedness of his work, and its integration in his capable hands, some justice has been done already; but a fuller reference may be made to two aspects of it. Both of these will be dealt with at length in subsequent chapters; but they must not be separated from the synoptic presentation with which we are here concerned. They are the ecumenical and the theological.

Some of Lidgett's best work for the union of the Anglican and the Free Churches was done in a series of informal meetings held at Lambeth Palace under the chairmanship of William Temple while Archbishop of York, meetings which produced the *Sketch of a United Church*, printed in 1935. Like Garvie and Jones of Bournemouth, and rather more pronouncedly than Carnegie Simpson, he was for meeting the Anglicans as far as he could in what followed from their views of the place of Bishops in the Church. Those private gatherings were, unhappily, no more successful than the numerous formal assemblies at Edinburgh and elsewhere. The reason however that made Lidgett a *persona grata* in Anglican eyes was not any readiness in him to surrender positions which Free Churchmen hold precious—far from it; it was the conviction which inspired all his work at the Settlement, that we are drawn together not by ecclesiastical formulae, or even by arguments on the essentials of the Christian Ministry, but by 'faith working by love', and by active co-operation rather than by consultations between differing religious bodies. If the Churches are ever to come nearer together, it will be by uniting in a common obedience to the law of the heavenly Father, who commands us 'to see and to serve', to combine the spirit of the High Priestly prayer of John 17 with the family prayer of Matthew 6, and to live and to act—how Lidgett loved to repeat the words—'as in heaven, so on earth'. A common churchmanship to him meant a common discipleship.

More important is Lidgett's theological writing. This too is considered in what follows. But it cannot be rightly appreciated unless it is linked with what sprang into light in the early days at the Settlement. The three treatises on which Lidgett's fame as a theologian chiefly rests were produced within ten years of one another, from 1898 to 1907. They were written for the most part during the mornings in the Settlement library, as the author marched up and down, dictating to his toiling secretary, or darting from one shelf to another to verify a reference, but advancing steadily with scarcely a pause. Only an hour or two would usually be allowed to this each day, along with the time he stole by the sea-side on a brief holiday, as John Wesley would sometimes steal a few days for retirement. 'An escape', some would comment, 'from the sombre duties of the Wardenship.' It was nothing of the sort. It was the assertion, in his thinking and writing, of what every hour at the Settlement was asserting in his active work; the 'sovereign Kingship' of God, who by His grace reveals Himself as the Father of men.

This is almost a commonplace today, until we try to work out how noun and adjective affect each other. But to assert it in the nineties as he did demanded courage of a high order. The ruling doctrine of the relation of God to man was shown, it was commonly held, in the penal aspect of the doctrine of the

Atonement. Dr R. W. Dale's assertion of this was upheld by most of the Methodist pundits; and the dismay and horror which followed any tampering with the traditional presentation of hell as the place of endless punishment, was shown in the excited discussion, in the Conference of 1902, of Dr Beet's denial that the Bible taught an eternity of conscious suffering for unrepentant sinners. Those who knew Lidgett when his Fernley Lecture was being written were aware of his nervousness lest his own view of the satisfaction of God there expounded— itself somewhat rigid to our present-day thinking—should be repudiated by the Methodist doctrinal authorities, and how galled he was when a review from which he had expected better things told him that he did not write like a sinner saved by grace.

The three treatises, *The Spiritual Principle of the Atonement, The Fatherhood of God* and *The Christian Religion*—they properly form a trilogy—are not only the statement of a theological or even a religious position. They are an *apologia pro vita sua*. How closely his theology dwelt by the inner springs of his life can be learnt from a remark which fell from his lips many years later. Five years after he had lost his son, killed while leading his company in an assault in the first World War, he published his commentary on the Epistle to the Hebrews. A friend was speaking to him appreciatively of the book. 'Yes', he replied, with a wistful look, 'he was a Captain, and a Son.'

If St Augustine's phrase, *pectus facit theologum*, ' 'tis the heart that makes the theologian', was true of any writer, it was true of Lidgett. He would have denied that he was a theologian *and* a social reformer. He was each because he was the other. To be drawn into the fellowship of the Father and the Son was to be drawn into the service of all for whom that fellowship was destined. It was 'to love them with a love like Thine'. And that love, so far from being a sentiment or a compartment of life, was, as with its divine and incarnate exponent, at once the flower and the fruit of the hardest thinking and the deepest experience. It was his life, because without it life would have fallen into fragments.

If this were more than a sketch of Lidgett's work, it would be

THE WARDEN OF THE BERMONDSEY SETTLEMENT 69

fitting at this point to refer to its limitations. The negative is often as significant as the positive in a man's life. We may learn from the empty spaces on the map no less than from the well-filled regions. In the carefully written autobiography to which reference has already been made, *My Guided Life*, there are only three mentions of the first World War which burst upon the country when he was at the height of his powers, and these merely speak of casualties. Of the deeper shadows which were already gathering above his head, the author says nothing. This was no accident. Ecumenical—the word was no favourite of his—meant for him the union of religious bodies within this country rather than the integration of all Christian men and women of every race and colour in the world for which Christ had died. He was never specially interested in the cause of what were called 'foreign missions', though he was entirely loyal to the missionary demands and projects of his Church, and championed them on occasion as few others could have done.

The truth is that he was born a Liberal, and remained a Liberal to the end. He was not indeed one of the old-fashioned Liberals, like Cobden and Bright, who fought for reform in the corn-laws and the franchise, but hated it—as Lord Shaftesbury knew so well—in the factory. But he was never affected by the expansiveness of Disraeli or Chamberlain or Lloyd George. To him the condition of England was the important thing; and he spoke or refrained from speech—no doubt, if pressed, he would have admitted it—as one who held that if the will of God were done in England, the rest would follow in its time. Thus, too, while a whole-hearted 'progressive', he never considered himself a member of the Labour Party. He had his friends among that party, such as Arthur Henderson; but throughout his life his closest associates politically were, like himself, middle-class men, who even if they came to acknowledge the Labour allegiance, retained the middle-class attitude, and were moved by the convictions which made Liberalism, at the turn of the century, the hope of all who longed for a worthier England. The progress he championed was progress within certain limits which he had no wish to overstep.

This accounts for the disappointment which he undoubtedly caused to some who had looked for a more aggressive leadership. He was untouched by the wave of pacifism which swept over this country, and more fiercely over France and America, in the years immediately before the outbreak of the second World War. He had little or no sympathy with the views on worship and the Lord's Supper advocated by the Methodist Sacramental Fellowship. He gave no support to the pleas for the admission of women to the Ministry; and on the thorny question of divorce he was all on the side of allowing the fewest possible facilities for breaking the marriage bond.

Throughout his life he was a true Gladstonian; though, unlike Gladstone, he never recanted an opinion or changed a position. But he was a Conservative in the sense in which Gladstone remained a Conservative, zealous to preserve all the gifts of the past, whether in his own Methodism or in the great Christian tradition of which he felt himself the heir, but ready and prompt so to interpret both gifts and traditions as to fit them to the constantly changing situations and demands of his times. Of this Liberal conviction one example, in the narrower field of ecclesiastical polity, was the scheme of Methodist Union as he shaped it; another, in the broader field of religious and social progress, was the comprehensive view of the service of God as he applied it alike to the streets of Bermondsey and the schools and institutions of the County of London.

But the parallel with Gladstone can be carried a stage farther. True, Lidgett could never have written *The Impregnable Rock of Holy Scripture*, or the Gladstonian studies of Homer; nor was he interested in art or literature or music so much as in making their treasures available for those from whom they had been hidden. But (and here was the strength of the Liberal tradition at its best) whatever he did was done 'because', as Mrs Gladstone once said of her husband, 'he believed that it was a duty owed by man to God', and, as Gladstone wrote after the 1880 election, 'it seemed as if the arm of the Lord had bared itself for work that He had made His own'. Such reflections as these may appear to carry us outside the scope of this chapter, but they lead, in reality, to the heart of its subject.

'There is no one in Methodism', we used to say, 'who can carry on the Settlement when Lidgett is gone.' That is true. Lidgett has gone, and the Settlement as he made it and knew it has come to an end. The Conference of 1954 decided that 'the Settlement building, while retaining the name, should be carried on as a part of the Bermondsey Mission'. This however must not be taken as a sign that there is no one in his Church with shoulders broad enough to wear the mantle that fell from him; or, now that the Warden is no more, that Methodism has no more reverence for his work. It is the duty of institutions to render themselves superfluous. That is an unpopular doctrine in governmental committees; yet to keep an institution alive for its own sake is to ruin it. Institutions are created to meet human needs, whether we think of the family (which, as someone wittily remarked, has succeeded in keeping itself alive with neither committees to govern it nor collections to support it), of the Church, or of the State; or, again, of political bodies, labour unions, or charitable organizations.

Some needs are permanent; and we shall never be able to do without the Church, the school, and the home, which exist to meet them. Others arise from circumstances which cry out for alteration; the more successfully the institutions function to which they give rise, the sooner their *raison d'être* will cease, and they will disappear. We may consider, for example, the ragged school, the workhouse, and the children's courts. The first, happily, exists no more; the need for it has vanished. The need that gave rise to the workhouse still exists, but in such a different form that the name is rightly used no longer. Children's courts still exist, because children still get into trouble; but when we have learnt what these courts compel us to take to heart, how to understand and prevent juvenile delinquency, the courts will go. All institutions in this second class, therefore, if worked properly, make for their own discontinuance. As for those that still remain, the fault, if it is a fault, is not theirs, but the society's which tolerate the needs they are there to meet.

How does all this apply to the Settlement? The previous pages should have made the answer clear. The need which the

Settlements were designed to supply—let us repeat it—was to bridge the gulf between the 'two nations', or, less inexactly, between the two halves of one nation. The existence of the gulf had been recognized for fifty years and more. By the middle of the nineteenth century the comfortable classes had done their best to forget it; but in the next thirty years, from 1850 to 1880, it had become tragically clear. As far as the majority in the Churches was concerned, attempts at relief had been made by spasmodic Christian charity. Unhappily, the remedy had proved more dangerous than the disease, and the angry cries for 'justice, not charity' had not brought the two classes any nearer together.

Thus the real remedy, it was felt, was for a larger influx from one section of the nation to the other. Human beings must be treated as human, not as mere recipients either of charity or of wages. Neighbourliness would produce knowledge, and knowledge would breed sympathy. The need would only, at bottom, be met by personal contacts. The score or two of Settlements which were formed provided for such an influx; but it was never more than rather absurdly small, setting a sprat, one might say, to catch a whale. Such a criticism, however, would be beside the mark. Many men and women who have served their day and generation have passed through the Settlements; and the emphasis on the need for personal knowledge and personal contacts first laid by the Settlements has influenced far more than the few thousands who at one time or another have been in residence. The Settlement conception, if not the Settlement embodiment of social service, is now taken generally as axiomatic.

Further, the literature inspired by this conception has been of immense influence. Following on the *Bitter Cry* and other similar revelations, came the eight volumes of Charles Booth's *Life and Labour of the People in London* (1902-3). These were followed by Seebohm Rowntree's *Poverty* (1901), a smaller parallel from York, more detailed studies of smaller areas like Warrington, and Alexander Paterson's *Across the Bridges* (1911), dealing with Bermondsey, and many others. The study of social conditions was growing fashionable.

A good deal that books could not do was accomplished, in the days before films, by the *Daily News* Sweating Exhibition, reproduced on a smaller scale in Birmingham (1906). All this failed to result in any large increase in the number of Settlements; but it meant that certain social conditions came to be felt as intolerable. A process of sympathetic and imaginative penetration has been at work. A new tone has appeared in twentieth-century legislation, and a new aim, by no means confined to the once powerful but now nearly defunct Liberal Party. The Labour Party still contains many members who once called themselves Liberals, and who have learnt the sting of poverty or the terror of unemployment through the kind of contact which the Settlements urged. Nor should the too quick despairers of our day forget that the impossible dreams of 1900, 'no destitute old age, no untended disease, no more recurrent unemployment', have become or are becoming the familiar achievements of today.

It is needless to go into further detail or to analyse causes and effects more closely. For better or worse, the twentieth century has discovered the State. The State is no longer to be satisfied with 'keeping the ring' or preventing acts of injustice or violence. It must take the place of the careless parent, check the heartless employer, and generally secure a reasonable measure of comfort for all its citizens. It is doing today far more than the founders of the Settlement movement ever hoped to accomplish by their modest technique; and the aims of the party in the LCC which Lidgett himself so vigorously led for twenty years have in many respects been more than fulfilled.

We need not stop to consider how much of this is due to the Settlements, to the general rise in the standard of Christian responsibility, to the emphasis on Christian citizenship in the Churches, or to the efforts and investigations that had their centre and inspiration in the great gathering in Birmingham in 1924 widely known as COPEC; nor need we decide on the other hand how much is due to the working of political parties, the women's vote, or the ambitions roused by the two great wars. Many would say that the State has done more than take the place previously filled by social endeavour; that the old clamant need for personal giving and serving is gone; and that the unbridged gulf of the eighties and nineties, and the means taken to bridge it, are now wholly out of date.

The Settlement activities are municipalized, and the amenities which the Settlements did their best to provide have been secured, or outmoded, by the car, the cinema, the wireless, cheap transport, and television. What was then out of reach for most is now within reach for nearly all. Moreover, the black spots of Charles Booth's map of London have mostly disappeared. Sir Llewellyn Smith's *New Survey of London Life and Labour* (1930, 1935), reads like the account of a different city. Even in 1902 Booth had noted that the worst of London slums had gone between 1866 and 1900; and, he asked, 'is it beyond hope that the thousand independent agencies that can be counted should recognize that they each hold a separate place in one great social movement?' Sir Llewellyn refers to the smaller proportion of the population habitually frequenting public houses and the large increase in the last thirty years of trained workers. The relations of young people of both sexes is healthier. 'Today', he writes, 'London poverty, in the sense in which Charles Booth used the term, is shown to have diminished to less than a third of its former proportion.' The rate of infant mortality in 1900 was 156; in 1928 it had shrunk to 68. In 1952 it was 27. The latest survey of Mr Seebohm Rowntree, with the assistance of Mr Laver, is entitled, significantly, not *Life and Labour*, but *Life and Leisure* (1949). Not only has the gulf, it would seem, been bridged, but the distinction between the 'two nations' has been well-nigh obliterated, in dress, amusements, holidays, education, and the availability of state services. The Children's Country Holiday Fund ought to be no more needed today than the Charity Organization Society. And if poverty still exists in 'pockets', local or social, the process of levelling up, or down, is still going on.

This can be illustrated by the transformation of charity, as we may call it. The fear and suspicion of charity, the dread of mere palliatives, so common in the writings of social reformers in the early days of the Settlement movement, are now rarely met with. The reason is that large portions of the field hitherto left complacently or despairingly to charity have been occupied, at least in this country, by the State. The relief of indigence, the care of widows and orphans, of the aged, of sick persons and young children, is no longer the care of voluntary agencies. The process, traditional in Great Britain for at least a century (it was really begun by the Poor Law of Elizabeth in 1601), by which the State cautiously takes over and then enlarges what private enterprise has first undertaken, is now almost complete. Many charitable societies have found themselves superseded; some have been drawn into co-operation with the State, or into activity under its direction.

Education is the most striking instance of this transference from the sphere of the voluntary to association with a public authority. But not less noteworthy is the way in which the State has taken under its wing the problem of the mentally and morally defective, with which voluntary associations, however efficient personally, could never expect to cope. The health visitor, the probation officer, the district nurse, the foster-mother in the approved home, are enlisted in a new army, as it were, in which the voluntary and the official elements have become mutually dependent, resting increasingly on State support and open increasingly to State inspection. There is hardly a charity which does not look hopefully for grants, and which does not anticipate a day when it will be told, or will tell itself, that it is no longer needed.

The effect of this far-reaching change is not to remove, but rather to emphasize the need for one thing at least which the Settlements set themselves to accomplish. The call today is for men and women qualified to work as paid public officers, who are also furnished with the zest that springs from a sense of vocation and is always ready to go the second and even the third mile, and who can combine the authority conferred by a public body with the patience, tact and sympathy of private and individual friendship. This demands just the training that can be supplied by a residential community living in the kind of neighbourhood where their delicate work is to be done. The danger today is not that social and personal needs will be neglected. The State will attend to all that. The danger is that these needs will be met in the wrong way; and that the paid servant will have to do what can only be done completely through the personal service and sharing inspired by the spirit of Christ, which is beyond money and price. As Lidgett wrote in the earlier days of the Settlement: 'In so far as I really love my neighbour, I love him as myself; that is, I treat him as having as just a right to well-being as I have myself, and am as ready to serve his well-being as to serve my own.'

The answer to our question, then, is not that the day of Settlements is over. What they set out to do has been done or is being done by other agencies than theirs. The arguments used by Lidgett in Cambridge or by Barnett in Oxford would now fall on deaf ears. But we must not be too hasty. That the need has passed would be true if the idea of the Settlement were interpreted in its narrower terms. If Settlements are to be simply a means to a kind of superior charity, securing amenities, as we call them, without the taint of degradation or inferiority, for those who would otherwise lack them, or enabling them to provide amenities for themselves, we can now turn our backs on their ideals.

But, as so often happens, the very circumstances that have closed one door for service have opened another. The spectacular advances toward the Welfare State have revealed its dangers: the loss of the sense of responsibility when the State is always there to step in; the desire for cheap and easy enjoyments, pushing a button or turning a switch, watching others rather than acting oneself; and the misuse of the newly found leisure. What must not be forgotten is that the State, the cause, if the indirect cause, of new perils, can do nothing to protect us from them. As a matter of fact, the fundamental remedy proclaimed by the leaders of the movement in the eighties was that the basis of all effective assistance is personal, and that all effective and personal giving is sharing, and sharing the real, that is, the spiritual values of life. This now needs more emphasis than ever. For in these days we are walking in an entirely new world, but a world in which the new perils must be met by the old principles.

For new perils certainly exist, even where the amenities provided by the State or purchased by higher wages are at their maximum. The young people of the higher-paid classes, with their wireless sets and cars, might be, as J. B. Priestley has put it, 'simply so many cave-dwellers for all the larger relations they have to the life of the community, or to the noble and enduring life of art, philosophy, and religion'. At the beginning of the century, a body of men or of women, living in a common residence with large rooms for differing kinds of social intercourse, was held to be the best device for such a life of sharing. Today, other devices are suggested—cells, priest-labourers, industrial chaplains. All of these have one recommendation, unhappily, to the *homme moyen sensuel*, in the Church or outside it: 'This means others and not me.' And they have the common fault of leading us to forget all the vast army of those who, in official or semi-official positions, are engaged all day in duties which can only be discharged in the spirit of the Settlement.

Something more, however, has passed away than the needs which could be supplied by the kind offices of residents in a Settlement. The whole complexion of religion has changed in this country. Anglicanism and Nonconformity as a whole no longer look at one another as actual or possible enemies in the political or educational world. But the Churches' hold on the mass of the people, to judge from their congregations, their Sunday-schools, and their adherents in general, has been weakened to a very serious extent; and there is a widening recognition, strengthened by the results of the two World Wars and the frightening menace of a world-wide and wholly irreligious Communism, that the hope of the future does not lie merely in the extension of social reforms or philanthropic activities, but in the penetration of the whole of our complex life by the convictions which rest at the heart of the Christian religion. Such a penetration can only be carried out by the action and leadership of Christian men and women, in politics, in education, in commerce and industry and municipal life, in the administration of the law, and (not least important) in journalism. It will at once demand and foster an intimate union between the religious denominations, a closer co-operation between all whom Charles Gore used to call 'men and women of good-will', and a firmer grasp of the essential connexion that binds Christian faith to Christian life and work, a connexion which can never be lost or surrendered save with fatal consequences to both. And to say this, as the previous pages have made clear, is to sum up all that Lidgett proclaimed in his words, his writings, and his life.

For the complete description of this spirit we may go back to the brief yet comprehensive statement, equally appropriate to his view of the Settlement and of every other movement that he guided, that 'the fatherly-filial relationship between God and man is at once the consummating gift and experience of the Christian life and also the key to the rational interpretation of the universe'—in other words, that the whole structure of human society is based on a common humanity in which each member is his brother's keeper, because that humanity is itself a family of which God is the Father and the Head. Every side of our life together as human beings can only be understood in the light of God's sovereign will for mankind. *Nihil humani alienum est a Deo*—nothing which touches us, or in which we touch others, but is in the closest touch with God. That Scott Lidgett kept this law through all the changing scenes of his life constitutes his unique claim on our admiration and our gratitude.

W. F. LOFTHOUSE

THE BIBLICAL THEOLOGIAN

CHAPTER THREE

THE BIBLICAL THEOLOGIAN

GOD sometimes honours his servants by accepting the price of their renunciations. When, along the winding road from Quy to Cambridge, under a stormy sky, the young Methodist divine renounced his 'philosophical and theological ambitions', that he might live among the London poor and demonstrate the practical power of Christian compassion in the darkest city of Victorian England, he counted a cost which, in fact, he paid. Henceforth the main energies of his virile frame and powerful intellect were diverted into other channels. Because he did in fact achieve intellectual eminence and renown, because no less than four great Universities honoured him with a doctor's degree in theology, we must not forget the price of his supreme vocation of public service. Because of it, the name of Scott Lidgett occupies less room in histories of Christian thought in the nineteenth century, though the more brightly written in heaven.

Yet though the renunciation was real, theology was for him the integrating fact. 'So far', he wrote, 'from my educational and other social activities having been a departure from this concern, they have been entirely based upon my construction of what is involved in the Christian revelation of God, and particularly of his Fatherhood.'

It was this wholeness of thought and action, based as it was upon the unities of Christian faith and experience, which underlay his great conception of 'Catholicity'.

He grew up in a self-contained Methodist world. 'Methodists, not Dissenters', he said of his grandparents; 'the doctrines in which we were instructed were the doctrines of the Catholic Reformed Church, with their Methodist emphasis.' There is a good deal of evidence, admittedly rather one-sided, to suggest that the temper of Methodist piety was more genial and optimistic than that of contemporary Evangelicalism. But it was a world which was rapidly opening up; the days when the mental horizon of Methodism could be squared by 'Our Doctrines', 'our discipline', 'our literature', and 'our hymns' were over. Under the sharp impact of Puseyite polemic, the Methodists were being impelled ever more rapidly along the road to the great alliance of Victorian Nonconformity, which was to reach a climax in the most fruitful decades of Lidgett's thought and activity.

This wider world, however, was a world in storm, a world where Christians faced a series of intellectual challenges such as had not been known since the crisis of the New Learning in the sixteenth century.

As in the age of Valla and Erasmus, so now, converging streams of new knowledge burst upon an unprepared orthodoxy, whose first reaction, naturally enough, was to go on the defensive, but whose fatal betrayal was to stay there. What had previously been virile, liberating impulses and intuitions, propounded by great minds and spiritual giants, had become cramped, rigid patterns of moralistic pietism. The new learning, in the nineteenth as in the sixteenth century, was not simply new information, but new methodologies, new ways of looking at the world as it is, and the past as it may have been, involving flexible adjustments of mind and spirit, not only toward the world of nature and history, but to the great imponderables of the invisible world. Thus the doctrine of evolution, potent no less in the fields of history and of philosophy than in that of biology, challenged a static conception of the universe to which, more than it knew, Protestant piety had become inured. The new attention to archaeology, the methods of historical investigation applied now to sacred history, the new interest in the creeds and practices of other religions, seemed to question the uniqueness of the Christian revelation, the veracity of the Christian Scriptures. And outside the Christian world, but pressing as never before on Christian consciousness, came the voices of doubt and unbelief, confident and truculent as never before.

Twenty years before, these things had brought to many Christians an almost intolerable tension. Lidgett grew into a world where there were already great allies at hand. The Victorian age of giants produced also giant Christians. Men might attack Christian doctrines and exclaim at apparent crudities in ancient orthodoxies, but they could not sneer at the mental and spiritual bankruptcy of Churches which produced a Newman, a Maurice, and a Dale. They might bring the partly justified charge of an other-worldly pietism against the Churches, but they could not press it right home to a generation which remembered Wilberforce, honoured Lord Shaftesbury, and heeded the passionate preaching of Charles Kingsley. Amid the hubbub about the Bible, there rose the mighty Cambridge trio, Lightfoot, Westcott and Hort, to witness that whatever foes the Christians may be expected to fight and even to fear, they need never be afraid of truth.

It is an impossible thing to diagnose the spirit of any age, to say what conditions its changing moods and temper, to say how much is owing to great thinkers and their books, how much to men of action, how much to the great impersonal forces which convulse a political or economic structure, and how much to the coral-insect-like achievements of millions and millions of ordinary people. Certainly we can recognize what somebody has called the 'phenomenon of simultaneous discovery', the way in which minds trained along similar lines, applying similar methods in a similar field of investigation, come within a short space of time to remarkably similar conclusions. It has been so in modern atomic research, something like it happened with the doctrine of Justification by Faith in the early sixteenth century, and something like it seems to have underlain what Lidgett called 'the Victorian Transformation of Theology'. The well-known case of the relationship between Maurice and Westcott illustrates the point. Striking as was the agreement between them, so that in exposition of the Gospel and in application of it Westcott might seem to be the disciple of Maurice, Westcott refrained from close attention to the writings of Maurice, not because he disagreed, but because he agreed so well.

Dr Fairbairn, in his essay, *Dale as a Theologian*, tells how 'A new spirit was being born within . . . evangelical theology. It may be described as a spirit less legal and more personal, less concerned with the abstract ideas of law and justice, and more concerned with the concrete ideas of fatherhood and forgiveness. Its earliest exponents had been men of Presbyterian birth and creed, notably Erskine of Linlathen, and Campbell of Row . . . but in all its forms it may be described as more a theology of Fatherhood than of Sovereignty.'

Fairbairn further suggests that Frederick Denison Maurice greatly enhanced the new tendency. Lidgett was more explicit: 'The restoration of the truth of the Fatherhood of God to its primacy in Christian thought and life was the greatest Theological and Religious achievement of the nineteenth century in this country. In bringing about this transformation, the influence of Maurice was the most important personal factor.' He was careful to point out, however, that there was something new and congenial to the temper of the changing age, which in part responded to, and in part conditioned, the new teaching. And in Lidgett's own case there is a personal pedigree.

There was, for example, the influence of his home. In his autobiography he paid moving tribute to the influence of his father. 'Indeed, I cannot help thinking that it has been owing to the subconscious influence of my father, taken away from us before I was fifteen years of age, that I owe the fact that my subsequent theological work has been directed to establishing and expounding the primacy of the Fatherhood of God as made manifest in the Incarnation of our Lord and interpreted by the Nicene creed.'

There were the fruitful contacts during his early ministry, with his beloved mentor, Dr W. B. Pope. Lidgett tells how he went a walk with the great Methodist divine who had just returned from shaping the new Methodist catechism. 'John Scott', he said, 'I have fought a great battle this week and won a great victory. You remember the first question and answer of the Catechism. "What is God?" "An infinite and eternal Spirit?" Well, I have got them to alter it, and now it is to be, "Who is God?" "Our Father".'

As we shall see, there was also the temper of Methodism, of the theology of John Wesley and the hymns of Charles, the 'optimism of Grace' of Evangelical Arminianism, which echoed to this emphasis, and which gives Lidgett a prophetic significance in the thought of his own Church. None the less, this was his own discovery, not less original because it responded to new currents in his age, or because others greater and more novel than himself were pointing in the same direction, saying the same things. Lidgett's own studies in historical theology confirmed the intuition, and it became plain to him that for long centuries the doctrine of Divine Sovereignty had been allowed to usurp the doctrine of Divine Fatherhood, with baneful results. The rich, deep, striking figures of the New Testament had been turned into theoretic patterns, as feudal, commercial, juridical conceptions had intruded, impersonalizing and depersonalizing the relations of men and God in the most holy and intimate of all Christian theodicies, forgiveness and Atonement.

Lidgett's own biblical studies, in the Johannine literature, the Epistles of St Paul to the Colossians and Ephesians, and the Epistle to the Hebrews, suggested a wider, richer balance of revealed truth, the unity of Incarnation and Atonement, of the life as well as of the passion of the Son of God, a union of creation and redemption which left nothing excepted from the range of Fatherly Love. This was the conception which with prophetic insight had been expounded by Maurice, and it offered easement, not only for Christians wrestling with the problems of the Gospel they preached, but for the daunting, baffling confrontation of the world outside, a faith hospitable, courageous, and daring enough to address with reconciling power the estranged traditions of the modern mind, in science, letters, and philosophy.

In these decades, therefore, it was natural that problems of Christology and Atonement should be considered afresh. A series of writers essayed a re-statement of Christian doctrine and tradition, determined not to surrender Scriptural truth, but also determined to meet old theological difficulties which had now ceased to be academic and had become for many an intolerable moral dilemma. Lidgett made a notable contribution to this creative ferment. Years of study and attentive reading went to the making of his greatest work, *The Spiritual Principle of the Atonement*, part of which he delivered as the twenty-seventh Fernley Lecture at the Leeds Conference of 1897.

The modern theological student would hardly suspect its revolutionary character. But there were leaders of Methodism who were suspicious and hostile toward the new doctrines. The greatest attack on Maurice had been written by the leading Methodist divine, Dr J. H. Rigg, in a work, *Modern Anglican Theology*, which trounced Maurice, Hare, Kingsley, Jowett, and their circle, through more than five hundred pages, and ran into several editions. It accused Maurice of corrupting evangelical truth with the infiltration of a cloudy Neo-Platonic mixture of rationalism and mysticism, most defective at the point of Atonement and Redemption. In fact, Rigg's very one-sided and on the whole obtuse study, though still of great interest and indeed importance to students of Maurice, illustrates the barrenness of the evangelical Augustinian tradition, which had emerged from the successive orthodoxies of Calvinism, Puritanism, and the eighteenth century full of dry bones, and badly in need of refreshment from those very streams of influence (the Greek Fathers, Luther) which Maurice found so congenial. Not that Rigg made much impression on Maurice's disciples. Lidgett told me that he had refused to read the book, a human sidelight on a young rebel at the only age in life when a loyal intolerance can be a mark of grace.

But the conservatives, and Dr Osborne their doyen, had the ear of Methodism. 'I was threatened', says Lidgett, 'by what is commonly called a "heresy hunt", for the publisher had, somewhat unadvisedly, supplied a copy of the proof to a clerical reviewer, who sought to stop the publication of the book by reporting its supposed heresies to the President of the Conference, the Rev. Dr Marshall Randles, Theological Professor at Didsbury College.' The teacher of theology in a theological college is always rather vulnerable to a charge of favouring deviationists from the party line, and as President of the Conference he upheld the view that Lidgett 'ignored the demands of divine justice and therefore the penal character of our Lord's sufferings; in addition—he shifted the emphasis from the Cross to the Incarnation, from the death to the life of Christ'. None the less, he refused to proceed to extremities, and Lidgett, on his side, had strong champions. The work was dedicated to Lidgett's great friend and theological patron, Dr Moulton, and immensely pleased Hugh Price Hughes, who secured for it an impressive review in the *Methodist Times.*

In an introductory chapter, Lidgett states the problem: What is the spiritual principle of the Atonement as a satisfaction for sin? The remainder of the work is occupied with his answer. The second chapter is an examination of the 'Historical cause of our Lord's death'. Lidgett does not begin, as he might have done, with the discussion of isolated texts in the Gospels, but gives an almost narrative assessment of the public career of our Lord. Doubtless this method of treatment owes something to the renewed attention to the life of Jesus and the circumstances of His ministry which was a feature of the time. What for Lidgett is of focal importance is the Sonship of Jesus in relation to the Divine Fatherhood; unlike a modern theologian, he is not primarily concerned with our Lord as 'Son of Man', Messiah, or with the Kingdom of God in an apocalyptic and eschatological setting. But he expounds the relationship of Jesus Christ to His Father as at once the ground of His unique authority, and as the grand cause of offence, stumbling and scandal, which led inexorably, through the growing hostility of ecclesiastical authority on the one hand, and His own perfect and unswerving obedience on the other, to His public execution. 'The historical cause of our Lord's death was His unwavering obedience to the Father, in the manifestation of the life of His Son.'

There follows a summary examination of the Biblical evidence, in Epistles, Acts, and Gospels, and a short discussion of three Old Testament themes—the 'Servant of the Lord', the sin offering, and the attitude of the Prophets toward sacrifice. In Chapter 4, 'Some theological accounts of the Atonement', he selects from the past, and also from the most notable contemporary discussion, certain positive principles in old theories which persisted in popular conceptions. He begins with Anselm, who so deeply influenced Western thought, and who massively affirmed the 'Godward' significance of Atonement. But Anselm is 'hampered at every point by his unsatisfactory conceptions of the relationship between God and Man . . . ; the analogy of a monarch and his subjects must in any case be seriously inadequate, but most of all that of a medieval monarch'. The result, in Lidgett's characteristically Methodist comment, is that 'the Cross is so explained as to stir no sense of wondering gratitude toward God as the author of salvation'. Next, Lidgett considers what he denominates the 'Calvinist Doctrine of the Active and Passive Obedience of Christ'—the distinction, sharpened through long Puritan debate in England, between the passive obedience of Christ in suffering and death, suffering which is the penal equivalent of our sin, and the active obedience of His life—a distinction which Lidgett affirms cannot be sustained by the appeal to the New Testament, and which, by concentrating on the death of our Lord as that which alone makes satisfaction for sin, empties the conception 'of all ethical significance, and is made repulsive by the exaggerated importance attached to suffering as such'. Grotius is interesting, not only as an Arminian divine who had greatly influenced such Methodist theologians as Richard Watson, but as firmly 'placing in clear light the character of God, the heinousness of sin, and the authority of the law'. The thought of the divine rectoral government of the Universe, and of the death of Christ not as fulfilment, but as relaxation of law, Lidgett declares to be defective and inadequate.

The discussion turns to contemporary writers, and first, Dr R. W. Dale, to whom Lidgett pays just and glowing tribute. But he fastens unerringly on a weakness which, in his later writings, Dale himself had tried to remedy, the establishment of an 'eternal law of righteousness', able to be considered as apart from the Divine Being. The result is that despite Dale's great and welcome emphasis on the Love of God as the over-arching principle of redemption, and on the relationship between Father and Son as central to any discussion of Atonement, the righteousness and goodness of God have become externalized. 'But',

Lidgett argues, 'faithfulness to the fellowship of love within the Holy Trinity, faithfulness to the ends of love in the relationship between God and creation, and, in both, faithfulness to the spiritual nature, which is love, is the meaning of the righteousness and goodness of God'.

McLeod Campbell stressed those aspects most neglected by Dale. For him, the satisfaction of Christ lies 'so exclusively in the Spiritual attitude of our Lord, that His sufferings seem to be almost accidental to it'. The sufferings of Christ are not penal, for 'the sufferer suffers . . . just through seeing sin and sinners with God's eyes'. In perfect penitence on behalf of humanity, Jesus confessed 'a perfect Amen in humanity to the judgement of God on the sin of man'. In effect, though Lidgett does not say this, Campbell's treatment, like a good deal of modern speculation, is a theodicy of Gethsemane rather than Calvary. Lidgett next briefly outlines the emphasis on Christ's self-surrender in the sermons of F. D. Maurice, and on the disciplinary value of His sufferings in the writings of Westcott. More extended treatment however is given to Dr Bushnell, who, Lidgett considers, externalizes the divine law even more grievously than Dale, and whose doctrine of the Wrath of God as almost an explosive passion is dangerously anthropomorphic. Bushnell's attack on the doctrine of satisfaction would be more credible, therefore, had not his own views such obvious weaknesses, barely offset by what Lidgett regards as his two great merits, 'the connexion between love and sacrifice', and the perception of the 'condition into which our Lord entered by the Incarnation, the full meaning and force of which was revealed on the Cross.'

The translation of the solid tomes of the theology of the great German divine, Albrecht Ritschl, were a major theological event in what, on other grounds, have been called the 'Naughty Nineties'. Lidgett in discussing Ritschl was therefore paying tribute to the latest theological fashion, as well as recognizing the importance of an impressive theologian. But despite brief and sharp criticism, there is one great point in common between the German and the English thinker. Both firmly agree that 'the relations between God and man are ethical, that ethics belong to a higher realm than law and government, and that therefore legal and governmental necessities cannot be treated as the supreme grounds of divine action'.

In Chapter 5, 'The Satisfaction of God', we come to the core of the great argument in a closely woven, logical exposition, which is never superficial and is often profound.

Scripture has shown a consensus that the Atonement has a Godward significance, that it consists in our Lord's endurance of death on our behalf, and that His obedience is of vital importance to the efficacy of His sacrifice. 'The question now is whether we can discover the rationale of this awful, yet gracious, divine dealing.' Lidgett affirms that the spiritual principle of the Atonement which conditions all the rest is the Fatherhood of God. For this he gives three reasons: it is the relationship which Christ has revealed; it is intrinsically the highest relationship, containing and controlling all others; and, third, 'the revelation of the Holy Trinity, and the constitution of the world in the Son of God, force us to treat this relationship as paramount'. It was a great misfortune that Socinianism caused the Puritans and Evangelicals to react against this over-ruling theme, and to fall back on 'Old Testament notions . . . profoundly modified by modern jurisprudence, political philosophy, and systematic ethics'.

The Fatherhood of God determines Atonement in two ways: 'first, as toward our Lord, the Son of the Father's love; secondly, as toward men, having their being in the Son, as the ground and Head of the race.'[1] That which makes the Atonement necessary is sin, with its consequences. 'The consequences of sin are wrath and punishment, of which death is the witness and the earnest.'[2] Lidgett seeks to rid the notion of the wrath of God from anthropomorphic associations, stresses that it is essentially altruistic, and finds an explicable analogy in the fatherly anger of a human parent against a rebellious child. The exposition which follows of death as a theological fact is profound and impressive. 'Just as there is throughout the universe the manifestation of life, so also throughout it there is

[1] op. cit., p. 243. [2] p. 263.

the anticipation of and the preparation for death. And death everywhere prevalent has its climax in man. And with man, death is present lifelong. There is not an interest of his in which it does not, though perhaps unrecognized, make its presence felt.'[3]

Against this sombre background of human disobedience and its fruits, our Lord's great, perfect obedience to the point of suffering and death is considered. 'Death, then, was the crown of our Lord's obedience, the supreme test applied to it.'[4] Here were all the conditions of 'filial satisfaction'. And if the question be asked, 'To whom was this satisfaction?', Lidgett powerfully recurs to the Trinitarian setting of his whole discourse, and to the Augustinian testimony to the unity of the whole Trinity in the work of redemption.[5] The death of Christ 'is vicarious, in the sense that He did for us that which was both necessary to be done and impossible for us to do'.[6] But, Lidgett insists, 'the vicarious nature of the Atonement does not bear the meaning that it is a case of simple substitution'.[7]

Christ is our life and head, the spiritual archetype of the race, as well as our representative, and because of these things He became flesh and blood, and not 'abstract, but unreal, humanity'.[8] Hence the wholeness of Atonement is only seen when we look beyond the act of satisfaction to the restored filial relationship, the new unity of men in Christ who is the origin and consummator of human destiny. This important and brilliantly executed argumentation is the real climax of the work. The remaining chapters, though important, are subordinate extensions, flying buttresses to the whole.

In the sixth chapter, the ethical perfection of our Lord is defended against some modern detractors, and is perhaps more 'dated' to modern readers who have to meet other objections to their faith than those offered aforetime by Strauss and T. H. Green. But Chapter 7, the relationship of our Lord to the human race, has a theme dear to the mind of F. D. Maurice and his disciple. The doctrine, with roots in the Epistles of St Paul and in the Logos doctrine of the Fourth Gospel, is an

[3] p. 260.   [4] p. 279.   [5] p. 282.   [6] p. 286.   [7] p. 288.   [8] p. 294.

affirmation of human solidarity in Christ, a solidarity which does not begin with the act of redemption: 'The place of Christ in redemption is due to His prior relation to the universe and man as their creator and sustainer.'[9] And if this be true when we look back to human origin, the same prospect opens out when we look forward along the plane of history: 'Christ stands out as the supreme fact of the human history which crowns the world, revealing and realizing the end toward which the whole creation moves.'[10]

This relation of the Son of God to humanity, while it does not impair or infringe the unity of the Holy Trinity, enabled His 'doing and suffering on our behalf' to become 'strictly representative acts', and enabled 'Him, and Him alone, to *give complete expression*, under our penal conditions, to the submission of mankind to God, to make reparation to His law, and to put away sin from man'.[11]

The next chapter, 'The Relation of our Lord's Divinity to the efficacy of the Atonement', is complementary. Athanasius, Anselm, and the Calvinist divines have given different answers regarding the importance in atonement of the Divinity of Christ, and some modern doctrines have introduced 'repulsive elements' at this point. But in fact, part of the answer lies in that very relationship of the Son of God to humanity which has already been expounded, for 'the relationships of the Son in the Godhead are the ground of His creative and constitutive relationship to mankind'.[12]

Moreover, our Lord's divinity 'conferred upon His sacrifice certain qualities of the greatest importance'.[13] It enabled God to 'put His own character in the clearest light';[14] it displayed His 'inflexible regard for the law, His unfailing demand for its fulfilment'.[15] And at the same time, the fact that God Himself has fulfilled the law shows 'that His demand is not a harsh and rigorous exaction', though in so doing He has in fact shown, as never before, the 'penal consequences of sin', and 'the immutability of those consequences'.[16]

Here the main argument is ended. The two closing chapters

[9] p. 355.   [10] p. 376.   [11] p. 378.   [12] p. 390.
[13] p. 393. [14] ibid.   [15] p. 394.   [16] p. 396.

are concerned with the application of the Atonement in the life of individuals—with justification by Faith, and the new life of sonship into which believers enter through the Blood of Jesus. Chapter 10, 'The Principle of the Atonement and Social Progress', is noteworthy, not so much for what it says, but for the fact that it exists, and it fittingly concludes the work. Here Lidgett decisively and wittingly breaks from evangelical individualism, with its overweighted emphasis on the conscience of the individual. He is too good a biblical theologian and too much a Methodist Preacher not to have given this aspect due weight in the preceding chapter, but he crowns his work by looking forward in the good Christian hope of a redeemed world, and in this he not only returns to historical Christian notes which had been mute too long, but ends on a genuinely prophetic note. That sublime 'appearing of the Sons of God' to which the whole creation, in the 8th of Romans, turns expectantly, is not the vision of innumerable individuals, but of a true City of God. The redeemed and restored filial relationship has immense practical consequence here on earth for social life. 'Sons of God, then brothers of one another, and spiritual heirs of the world—this is the irresistible logic of the Christian life, and in it is the security for all true human progress.... The fuller realization of the filial spirit will have its immediate effects upon political, social, and economic interests, ordering them in growing conformity to the mind of Christ.'[17]

On this note the work ends. 'The world will never be transformed by calling forth or organizing new forms of selfishness to redress the balance of the old. The greater selfishness of the greater number might be a more destructive tyranny than any which has passed away. Only by the law of service, ungrudgingly rendered in free spirit to God on behalf of men, at the cost of the self-sacrifice which is the price of love and righteousness alike, can the progress of mankind be secured. The principle of our Lord's death is both the end and the way.'[18]

The Spiritual Principle of the Atonement is Lidgett's greatest creative writing, and we have given it an extended treatment

[17] p. 415.   [18] pp. 415-16.

because into it are woven those great principles which underlay all his later work, and which recur again and again in all his writings. To read it today is to wonder whether it has not deserved rather better of posterity than it has received, been too little regarded outside the Methodist world which received its main impact. There may be reasons for its limited and transitory hold upon theological attention. A good deal of what he had to say was, as we have seen, already being said. Profundity and originality were more engagingly combined, before Lidgett's work, by Dr Dale, and afterwards, by W. H. Moberley. Lidgett's reasoning is close knit and logical, and his style attains again and again an Augustan poise and balance, but there are no fireworks. Moreover, though lucidity became a hallmark of his later utterances, there are parts of the argument where, as with F. D. Maurice, the great Christocentric affirmations seem to cloud the issue. Despite their crudities, the old analogies of evangelical tradition were clear-cut and did offer some succinct, if finally unsatisfying, rationale of the Godward significance of atonement. In reducing the emphasis on the penal element, and in drawing back before a conception of vicarious penitence such as W. H. Moberley was so powerfully to examine, Lidgett falls back on the majestic, but comparatively intricate doctrine of the Son of God as Head of the race. Moreover, he introduces at major points in his argument the analogy of the parent and child. This is never exaggerated and is used with restraint and force. But one wonders whether this is not a mistaken method of applying the spiritual principle of Divine Fatherhood to Atonement. It has often been noted that nearly all the historic theories of Atonement have employed some key figure which responds to the spirit of the age, as feudal monarchy in the time of St Anselm, and international law in the time of Grotius. Might it not be suggested that similarly in the setting of nineteenth-century England, the analogy of the Family and of the Victorian Parent has a similar origin? And might not a really thoroughgoing Biblical Theology, while not abandoning these useful illustrations, have concentrated, for its exposition of the Fatherly principle, upon that relation between Father and Son reflected in the words, work, and witness of Christ in the Gospels (and especially in this connexion, explicitly stressed in the Fourth Gospel), with all the consequences of these biblical illuminations for the state of man? However these things may be, Lidgett's book courageously expounds what we may call the Divine priorities in the doctrine of Atonement, and offered easement of conscience to many thinking Christians to whom the evangelical clichés had become intolerable. And if there are gaps in his attempted 'rationale', he fails at the point where all others have come short. If he stumbles, it is because he is really on the heights of the great argument, and if to a modern mind he seems only to have reached Camp 5, we remember that this Mount Everest of history and theology is something which *homo viator* can never fully apprehend or explain.

Lidgett's next work complements his examination of Atonement. Published in 1902, it is a full-scale exposition of the *Fatherhood of God*. And here there is no doubt about its being a thoroughgoing biblical theology. All the New Testament evidence is carefully examined, in terms of the best critical scholarship available, and Lidgett has room and leisure to expound what he had perforce to take for granted in his earlier work, the doctrine of the Universal Fatherhood of God, as against those who would limit that benevolence to the elect or to believers. He is able, moreover, to meet the criticism which he had noted earlier, of those who affirmed that Fatherhood is only one among many, and not even the primary quality of God in the Biblical revelation. In a careful exposition of Old Testament doctrine he puts the case that in fact, Fatherhood is the grand all-inclusive biblical doctrine of God in relation to men, and that it fully comprehends His sovereignty, His kingly rule over men, His justice, and His control over creation. A long chapter on 'The Historical Development in Christian History' simply expands his earlier affirmation that Sovereignty had, from the Middle Ages onward, usurped the place of Fatherhood in Christian theology. What he has to say about historical theology, apart from this point, is not remarkable, though the striking appreciation of Dante is a reminder how the writings of Newman, and the 'Divine Comedy' of

Dante, were late Victorian enthusiasms, not only among high Anglicans and Catholics. Though, as I say, Lidgett's comments on historical theology have little survival value, there is one exception. Everything he writes about Methodist history and the significance of its history and theology is well worth reading, and is often profound and important in its insight. That is true of the two or three pages which begin with page 268 of this book, a discussion which recurs at page 333. Here he stresses the doctrine of the Holy Spirit as that about which the Methodists brought a new proportion of truth, if no original ideas, and he stresses the experience of 'Sonship' which was the foundation of their evangelical testimony, 'what the early Methodists meant by describing their new experience as "stepping into liberty". The phrase set forth the buoyancy, the spiritual power, the sense of heirship which belong to those who come to realize their sonship.'[19]

And this work, too, ends with the prospect of a divine consummation, of opening horizons, which have relevance for this world order. 'That (man) must have a sufficient and abiding universe, fitted to his spiritual conditions; and that he belongs to *this* universe, and cannot, even in imagination, be transported to another; that therefore he is to look to its transformation, and not to its abandonment as a waste product, in order to the creation of a new one—all these propositions are bound up with the hope of the consummation of all things, as set before us in the New Testament.'[20]

This is the work from which Hugh Price Hughes made his last sermon, and in his last conversation with Lidgett, he told him that 'in his opinion my books had finally disposed of the juridical view of redemption'.[21] It was widely used as a text book, not only in Methodist colleges, and was the occasion of the award to Lidgett of the D.D. of Aberdeen. No theological writer as concerned with his contemporary vocation as Lidgett could be content, however, simply to expound Christian doctrine. There was too much clamant unbelief in the world outside, and a defensive spirit in some quarters in the Churches. At no time since the intellectual storms burst in the beginning of

[19] *Fatherhood of God*, p. 336.   [20] ibid., p. 419.   [21] *My Guided Life*, p. 160.

the Victorian Age, could or can the Church abandon the task of apologetic and explanation.

That Lidgett's expositions of doctrine rest upon foundations which are congruous with the facts of the natural and historical order, that they are reasonable, and that the Christian claim to be a final and universal religion is valid—these are the theme of his third volume, *The Christian Religion, its Meaning and Proof*. In this work, Lidgett uses his wide reading to good effect, and reveals a philosophic equipment of which only glimpses had been given in his earlier works. Most original of all is the central core of the book, which is an exposition of the nature of religion itself, and an examination of the leading non-Christian religions. Again, much of what he has to say is no doubt dated, and the last fifty years has brought an immense re-valuation in the field of Comparative Religion. The third part of the work is an examination of Christian evidence, a criticism of philosophic agnosticism, a re-statement of the argument from Design, a sketch of the Christian doctrine of Man and of Redemption, and an exposition of the Christian doctrine of the nature of God, leading to the final affirmation that it is the 'Fatherhood of God' which affords the 'indispensable, complete and only explanation of the meaning and end of the Universe'.

This third work of Lidgett seems more dated than the others. It was addressed to a cogent contemporary apologetic, too 'topical' to endure. And perhaps the pressure of other activities was becoming evident, for on the death of Hugh Price Hughes Lidgett had felt the need for an even more urgent dedication to public and ecclesiastical affairs.

The three major works of Scott Lidgett we have described brought out his best gifts, his originality, his clarity, his power for sustained and reasonable argument. They made genuine impact upon the Nonconformist theological world, and they spoke acutely to the condition of the time. It has frankly to be admitted that, save to the student of historical theology, they have little survival value. On the other hand, the two succeeding studies, which are biblical expositions, are still well worth reading. Our age has recovered a lost taste for theological exposition, for a biblical commentary which is not simply content to discuss problems of textual, literary, historical, and psychological criticism. Moreover, in regarding the doctrine of Divine Fatherhood as a master key, Lidgett employs by anticipation the modern Swedish methodology of 'motif research', and one is inclined to think that, given a Swedish name, its lucid English broken up, and the 'dated' pieces of critical discussion removed, a reprint of Lidgett's work would find a timely place in modern discussion—a point to which we shall more seriously recur at the conclusion of this present essay.

The first of the two volumes, *God in Christ Jesus* (1925), is a study in the Epistle to the Ephesians. The opening passages which discuss the authorship of the Epistle lag inevitably behind recent technical discussion in our own time. But the body of the work is an exposition of the breath-taking sweep of the Divine purpose revealed in Jesus Christ, and made plain through the Church. The first half of the book, with a striking examination of the Doctrine of the Spirit, describes the 'unbounded possibilities' of salvation, the limitless horizons opened before mankind in the divine purpose. The second half is concerned with 'The Christian Commonwealth'—a phrase which would have delighted Martin Bucer and Oecolampadius, the two Reformers who like Lidgett were really at home with this Epistle. For Lidgett's practical Churchmanship was rooted in his great doctrines, and the Epistle to the Ephesians is the place above all in the New Testament where the inner connexion between Fatherhood, Sonship, and the life of the Christian in the Church and in the world is made plain. Writing no longer against the background of an age of confidence, but under the shadow of that first World War which ushered in a new 'Age of Violence', Lidgett's climax is still one of Christian hope, still an optimism of Grace.

'The assurance that "God shall be all in all" contains the promise that love shall be triumphant. This means that Christ guarantees the future of the universe as a whole, all the higher values that are attained in its history, and in particular all the personalities in whom these higher values are realized. The glory of God is revealed in the perfection and permanence of

His work. His work can only be perfected and be permanent in His Sons.'[22]

'It appears to me', wrote Lidgett in 1934, 'that insufficient attention has been paid by Christian thought to the Epistle to the Hebrews. Expositors have been too much occupied by the superficial features of its doctrine of the Priesthood and Sacrifice of our Lord as the ideal reality of which the Levitical system was the preparatory shadow. Hence they have failed to apprehend and do justice to the deeper teaching as to the Sonship of our Lord.'[23] Thus *Sonship and Salvation* (1921) attempted to apply the great *motif* of Divine Fatherhood to the Epistle to the Hebrews. Lidgett does with 'Sonship' in this great Epistle what for some of us Alexander Nairne did with 'Priesthood' in his *Epistle of Priesthood* (also a study in the Epistle to the Hebrews). As Lidgett expounds the great conceptions of the Epistle, he brings to his portrayal the fruits not only of study but of devout meditation. This is biblical theology, allowing the Bible to explain itself, in its own words and categories, and out of that deep inner unity which it is no mere remnant of old-fashioned orthodoxy to recognize. It is good, solid fare, with no concessions to our modern appetite for epigram and illustration. And like the study in Ephesians, it well repays re-reading.

At the end, in the grand Maurician manner, Lidgett returns to the great Christological vision and to the Blessed Trinity. 'Without prejudice or injury to His absolute perfection and eternal blessedness, God realizes His eternal purpose through and for His Son. He realizes eternally in Himself all that He brings into becoming throughout the course of history. . . . The creation, redemption, and perfecting of His sons is thus, in the last resort, an activity within, and not outside of, His own perfect life.'[24]

It was with immense pleasure that, in 1934, Lidgett accepted the invitation to give the Maurice Lectures at King's College, London. The little book in which these lectures were published contains a valuable and compressed diagnosis of the Victorian

---

[22] p. 367. [23] *Victorian Transformation of Theology*, p. 87.
[24] *Sonship and Salvation*, p. 255.

scene a century ago, and describes the transformation of the whole theological climate which occurred as the result of many influences, but among which the influence of Maurice may well have been the greatest single human factor. The paragraphs in which Lidgett appraises Maurice and outlines his theological stature are still the best paragraphs which have so far been written about him. 'I regard Frederick Denison Maurice as having been by far the most important and significant personality—the most potent and pervasive influence—in the religious life and thought of England during the last century. A very great man, he owes his pre-eminent importance and influence to his marvellous—I am inclined to say unique—combination of prophetic witness, systematic thought, and creative endeavour, unified and inspired by the ceaseless aspiration and pursuit of a wholly consecrated and truly saintly life.'[25]

It is a pity that Lidgett did not devote more than one lecture to the systematic exposition of Maurice in his own terms, for had he done so, his book would have been a pioneer study of great importance. As it is, the remainder of the book works out Lidgett's own great affirmations which, as he rightly stresses, were also Maurice's deep biblical insights, but which the student of Lidgett's earlier writings will know very well. And in fact, Lidgett had already confessed in writing *Sonship and Salvation*: 'With the completion of this book, my theological task, for whatever it may be worth, has been finished. From first to last it has been concerned with the Fatherhood of God, as revealed in our Lord Jesus Christ.'[26]

Though this in the main was true, and Lidgett did not in fact in his later writings develop many new truths, his Beckley Lecture (1938), *The Idea of God and Social Ideals*, enabled him to make clear the connexion between his theology and his public and social work, though by this time the Christian concern for the social implication of the Gospel was less novel than a generation before. In some ways the work is very typical of theological utterances in the 1930s. There is the inevitable quotation from Whitehead, and the name of God in the Old

---

[25] *The Victorian Transformation of Theology*, p. 13.   [26] op. cit., Preface, p. 8.

Testament, which, rendered as 'Jehovah', had done pretty well for the hymns of Watts and Wesley, and had been so rendered in Lidgett's *Fatherhood of God*, had now to be rendered 'Jahweh'. There is not much that is striking in the historical and theological argument of the book, though again, there is one exception to be made. Whenever Lidgett touches the Methodist Revival, the work of the brothers Wesley, or the history of Methodism, his are golden words, to be pondered seriously, since many of them are wise with an older, deeper wisdom than that of our present generation. Thus he offers a penetrating critique of Whitehead's saying that 'Methodism was singularly devoid of new ideas, and singularly rich in vivid feelings'. With that humour which rarely got into his prose, but which was a deep trait in the man, Lidgett remarks that Whitehead's words about 'rich feelings' would most likely be only too congenial to many Methodists. And then he adds a comment which perhaps applies to his own work as well as to that of John Wesley: 'Wesley inherited the great tradition of New Testament, Catholic, and Reformed theology. He accepted its doctrines, emphasized their meaning, and for the most part moved within their boundaries. Yet the quality of "newness" extends beyond "new ideas". There may be a new emphasis, a new proportion, a recovery of what has been neglected and become obscure, which may effect as true and vital a revolution as the importation of new ideas from without. Such newness was characteristic of Wesley's teaching.'[27]

The remainder of Lidgett's writings is of two sorts. There are little books of devotional meditation, not sentimental enough, or enlivened sufficiently with illustrations and anecdotes, to have made them best sellers, but rather closely knit expositions of scriptural truth about the great doctrines of the New Testament.[28] Some of them were written in his great age, but there is no faltering of the lucid style, which in his maturity enabled him to give to an extempore speech a classic form such that it might be printed forthwith, a test which few utterances of his successors could meet.

[27] *The Idea of God and Social Ideals*, p. 82.
[28] *The Cross* (1941), *The Crowns of Jesus* (1941).

The other works are occasional writings and speeches. His essays in the *Contemporary Review* were published in 1943 as 'God in the World—Essays in Christian Theism'. They reveal how deep and wide and constant was his reading not only of classical theology but of contemporary thought. The subjects range from the celebration of the English Bible (his fine essay on Bede appeared in another commemoration volume) to a critique of William Temple, of Barth, and of the Ecumenical Movement. More important than his essays were his sermons. Though we are not here concerned with Lidgett as a preacher, we cannot but regret that his gift of illustration, his occasionally devastating power of trenchant epigram, and his humour, did not intrude into his more serious theological compositions. In the sermons, however, there is a trait which is of cardinal importance in any proper assessment of his theology.

In his work on Maurice, Lidgett had said: 'His doctrine of God was founded upon and inextricably bound up with the Catholic Christology of the Incarnation. He worked not only *upon*, but *within* this great inheritance.'[29]

This also was true of Lidgett. It was, rather oddly, his grandmother and an aunt who had first directed him to the study of Newman. 'I became in my early ministry, a careful reader of his writings, and in particular my attention to the Nicene controversy . . . was turned into a subject of careful study.' Lidgett's theology found supreme liturgical and confessional expression in the Nicene Creed. Here he was at home. Here in later years he found his theme for memorable discourses on the Mighty Acts of God, and he was happiest of all when, among his own brethren, he could weave into them the hymns of Charles Wesley. In his age, shortly before he retired from the Chairmanship of the South London District, his deafness, and an inherent inability to suffer fools gladly, which in the latter days could not always see to distinguish the sheep from the goats, made some of the Superintendents restive, and roused the younger men. But if the May Synod was held at Ascensiontide, as he seemed often to contrive that it should be, there would be from Lidgett an unforgettable exposition, extempore

---

[29] *The Victorian Transformation of Theology*, p. 38.

and for forty minutes, of the Kingship of Christ, reaching its true magnificent climax in Wesley's 'Rejoice, the Lord is King!'

Nobody who saw it would ever forget his last great public utterance, when he delivered the oration at a service commemorating the Wesleys, in the Church of St Mary the Virgin, Oxford, and before the World Methodist Conference. The Nicene Creed was on the order of service, and well before the appointed time he began to rise slowly, painfully, to his feet, in time to be upstanding for a moment as important as 'The Queen' to some ancient Captain of the Guard. The acoustic aids broke down during the address, but many who stood too far away to catch its argument bore away with them as a precious and indelible memory, the recurring refrain of the now and again uplifted voice—'The Brothers Wesley . . . but especially John'.

Of the place of Lidgett in the history of Christian thought time is likely to be an inexorable judge, and he would not thank us for sentimental exaggeration of his importance. But he was a great man, and one element of his greatness lay in the fact that he combined real statesmanship in action with what Dr Wilbert Howard called 'the statesmanship of thought'. He is a sign and a portent to those who are constrained to combine study with an active ministry, or with the growing pressures of public affairs. In the realm of the invisible he moved among truths too big to allow of any cramped or sectarian expression. He reminds us that to do great things we must be ourselves apprehended by great truths. And perhaps we shall find the secret of true Churchmanship not so much in the study of ecclesiology as in devotion to the Blessed Trinity, among those heights and depths from which here and now all the separated Churches draw their true life. The great Christological passages of the Epistles were not for Lidgett mere peripheral mental furniture from which a man might make his sermons, but springs of action moving heart and will.

There are few original ideas. His master themes he confessed to have learned from others, and above all from F. D. Maurice. But there is in him a new proportion of truth, something which was of a piece with his own spiritual pedigree, the Evangelical Arminianism of the earlier Methodists and of the Wesleys. Lidgett as a thinker belongs to the Victorian and Edwardian age. He had no understanding of the Continental context which made Barth a prophetic witness after the first World War—and in fact he had a way of lumping Calvinist and Lutheran Fathers together in a way which would make a German theologian's hair stand on end. His balance of faith and reason, and his firm grasp upon certain fundamental Christian dogmas, look back rather perhaps to the age of Westcott, Lightfoot, and Hort, than forward to our modern problems. Yet the question arises whether a new interpretation and adjustment of Maurice might not represent an English theological contribution of importance to the ecumenical conversation. And when we turn to the intricate and exciting field of modern Biblical Theology, we may wonder whether the time is not overdue for some return to the themes of Fatherhood and Sonship. The eschatological setting of the doctrine of the Kingdom of God, the importance of the apocalyptic background in the time of our Lord with its baffling but intriguing literature, the wider issues raised by questions of 'De-mythologizing'—all these are of importance in their own right, and there can be no retreat to an earlier period. But it is already apparent that behind a good deal of apparently technical discussion there are dogmatic patterns, persisting principles and assumptions taken from Calvinist and Lutheran and Catholic orthodoxies, all of them rigid and to some extent one-sided. There are evident strains in the ecumenical discussion at this point. The Methodists may have no giant theologians, no original ideas to contribute, but they have within their pedigree a proportion of truth, a temper which derives its optimism of Grace, not from secularized humanistic assumptions about progress, but from the victorious affirmations of the New Testament. The Divine Fatherhood and the Sonship of Christ, the sonship of the redeemed, the great apprehension of the cosmic as well as the historical scope of the Work of Christ—here are frames of reference which might bring refreshing readjustments to Christian thought in our day, not least in relation to the mission of the Church in an estranged modern world. Certainly any such Methodist discussion would need to begin with the clues provided in the writings of Scott Lidgett.

Finally, we must stress the importance to him of the conception of 'Catholicity', which is John Wesley's 'Catholic spirit' interpreted in the modern age, and in which all the great doctrines we have outlined cohere. None served his denomination more fruitfully or did more important public service to the cause of the Free Churches. Yet none drew attention more forcefully to the dangers of sectarianism. To a lady who once said half apologetically, 'Of course, you know I am a Congregationalist, not a Methodist', he replied with a smile: 'That's right, you're like me, a Catholic.'

In 1907 he thus addressed the Free Churches: 'Catholicism has been the worst foe of catholicity. Denominationalism, if exaggerated, may be equally fatal. An exclusive spirit toward men, whether of other Churches or of no Church, whether of Christian or non-Christian races, will shut us out from knowing in all its fullness the grace of Christ and from manifesting it in all its power to our fellow men.'[30]

And in perhaps his greatest utterance, his Presidential address to the Methodist Conference in the following year, he said: 'Not a saint, a thinker, a hero, or a martyr of the Church, but we claim our share in his character, influence, and achievements, by confessing the debt we owe to the great tradition which he has enriched by saintly consecration, true thought, or noble conduct. ... The schismatic is always a traitor. Most of all is he such in the present day. Methodism, if true to its original spirit, ... will not fear a closer partnership with all them that love our Lord Jesus Christ in sincerity.'[31]

He spoke then words which stand today as a prophetic challenge to the Church: 'We are here today humbly, yet confidently, to affirm our share in the great Catholic inheritance of the past. Who, save ourselves, can separate us from it?'

GORDON RUPP

---

[30] *Apostolic Ministry*, Chaper 15 ('Catholicity the mark of Spirituality'), p. 281.
[31] ibid., Chapter 1 ('The Catholicity of Methodism'), pp. 13-16.

THE EDUCATIONIST

CHAPTER FOUR

THE EDUCATIONIST

IT is not without significance that Scott Lidgett lived during the hundred years when the State's view of education changed from one of complete indifference to one of supervision and then to one of direction. In 1854 the Government was beginning to realize that it must take responsibility for the education of the nation's children and for the social betterment of an increasing number of its people. It was in 1854 that John Scott Lidgett was born, and during the following ninety-eight years he was circuit minister; founder and Warden of the Bermondsey Settlement (1890-1949); a member of the London School Board (1897-1903); a member of the LCC Education Committee (1905-28) and for part of that time Deputy Chairman of the Committee; a representative of the LCC on the Governing Bodies of various Schools, Colleges, and Polytechnics; Senator of the University of London (1905-28); a member of the Methodist Education Committee; Secretary of a number of special Committees set up by the Connexion; President of the National Free Church Council (1906); President of the Wesleyan Methodist Conference (1907); President of the Free Church Federal Council; first President of the united Methodist Church (1932); Governor of The Leys School, and of Southlands, Westminster, Queen Mary and the Royal Holloway Colleges; Chairman of the Quarry Centre for Psychotherapy, Epsom; Chairman of the Universities' China Committee; Vice-Chancellor of the University of London. And these are only some of the high offices which he held directly or indirectly connected with education.

Scott Lidgett has been described as a pioneer, especially, of course, in regard to his work at Bermondsey. Without belittling him in any way, it might be better to consider him as a particularly able exponent and executant of the rapidly developing spirit of his age. He had too orderly a mind to be a pioneer in the usually accepted sense of the word. Throughout his life he wrote articles on current topics and reviewed books, especially for the *Contemporary Review*, and this orderliness of mind manifests itself clearly in these writings. So often, after a searching and revealing introduction to his topic, he writes: 'A survey of the whole situation appears, to me at least [for he was always humble], to lead to the following conclusions. . . .' He would then tabulate clearly and concisely what those conclusions were. This trait of his character and intellect was seen in similar fashion in his committee work. As Chairman of some committee he would briefly introduce the subject for discussion, would listen (often seemingly half asleep behind his unforgettable steel-rimmed spectacles) to members of the committee expressing their far from lucid views, and then would sum up in the manner which no one who sat with him could forget; no detail that was significant was missed, no irrelevance was included. The issue was made clear-cut, and however wordy had been the discussion, the Chairman's summing up presented a logically developed theme on which a vote could be taken. These qualities were not developed without hard work. However comparatively unimportant the committee on which he served, he would spend a great deal of time going carefully through a meeting's agenda the night before, and this was particularly noticeable in his later University work. He was always punctual, and nothing exasperated him more than unpunctuality in others; he had a sense of ritual which grew more pronounced as he grew older. There had to be order in everything.

All this may appear to have little to do with education, but it is the disciplined mind of clear perception, quick grasp, and logical thought which is needed in the good schoolmaster, the good administrator, the good statesman. Scott Lidgett was never a schoolmaster, but he guided schoolmasters and he taught them, and that is often more difficult than teaching children. Amid the welter of new ideas which were beginning to take shape in action at the close of the nineteenth century, when it must have been especially difficult to discern the merely idealistic from the potentially practical, Scott Lidgett steered a straight course—because he had trained himself to set out clearly in his own mind the various factors, to select the crucial, and to reach a logical conclusion on the basis of which plans could be made and action taken. That ordered attitude of mind is revealed again and again in all his undertakings, and accounts more than any other factor, except of course his own personality, for the ease and success of his chairmanship of difficult committees. He hated untidiness of mind, however human he may have been over untidiness in other directions—in his own study for example. He disliked especially two kinds of people: the hard-boiled and the woolly. He met both all too frequently, and on his return to the privacy of his room he would explode about some particular person who had offended in one of these ways.

It has been well said that education is the dynamic side of philosophy, and history and biography suggest that no man, whatever the depth or the breadth of his intellect, has so fully formulated a philosophy of life as to see his own place in the working of society until he has reached the age of thirty. So it was with John Scott Lidgett. Shy, diffident, yet from an early age thrown into contact with challenging experiences and influential personalities,[1] he was content to be a lone wolf, a fighter. His very lack of training in a theological college, as he himself confessed, 'left me to face the many problems, spiritual, intellectual, and practical, which confronted me, in loneliness, and to discover for myself, often with great soul travail, such solutions as henceforth supplied the basis of my thought and practical endeavour'.[2] He had the gift, nowhere better evidenced than at the Bermondsey Settlement, of making other people feel that they belonged to the work in hand and that no effort was too great; he had a capacity for giving a dynamic quality to everything that interested him and for infecting others. But his was not, in the early days at least, a magnetic personality—formidable, perhaps, because apparently rather humourless, though as he grew older he grew gayer and less narrow.

[1] See his own chapter on 'Formative Influences' in *My Guided Life*.
[2] op. cit., pp. 76-7.

His was the sort of personality and calibre of intellect which would have carried him to the forefront of any profession. Here we are considering how it came about that a Methodist minister became Vice-Chancellor of the world's largest University, how it was that leaders of Church and State came to consult him on matters of education. Seeds were certainly sown when he was a mere toddler. As he later recalled, that band of educational and Nonconformist pioneers who in the face of outspoken and often bitter criticism built a Methodist Training College in the slums of Westminster made an impression upon him as a child which he never forgot. To quote his own words: 'The whole atmosphere of the College was dominated by a serious sense of calling which was common to both tutors and students. Serious serenity, cheerful confidence, reverent dedication prevailed in a dominant temper of at-homeness and comradeship. This atmosphere was largely created and sustained by John Scott',[3] who was Scott Lidgett's maternal grandfather. President of the Wesleyan Conference for the first time in 1843, the Rev. John Scott led the cause of Methodist education throughout his life; an authoritative councillor in all affairs of Wesleyan Methodism, he became recognized far beyond the bounds of the Connexion as a great ecclesiastical and educational statesman. At his home the young John Scott Lidgett spent many months of his childhood; at his hands the boy of fourteen received his first Communion only a few days before his grandfather's death at the age of seventy-six. 'Christian devotion, high integrity, ripe sagacity, fatherly influence, were the outstanding marks which made him so widely and powerfully influential throughout the arduous years in which he served his own generation by the will of God.' These are the words of the grandson.

Other men, more distinguished theologians, came to have their clear influence upon the young man. One can read of these formative influences and personalities in Scott Lidgett's own books, but great as his debt was to them, it was to John Scott that he turned again and again as his path led him to the wider fields of education and politics and statesmanship. But

[3] *Westminster College Bulletin*, August 1944.

first he travelled the road of every Methodist minister. He answered the call to the Ministry in 1876 at the age of twenty-two. When he was appointed immediately to the Pottery Circuit of Tunstall, and went there from the comparative respectability of Victorian London as a graduate of its University, the shock must have been unpleasant, however beneficial history may acclaim it. Startled by the artificial and often unwholesome emotionalism of North Staffordshire revivalism, yet warmed by the hospitable and kindly nature of the folk, he gained an insight into their ways of thought and the actual working lives of the miners and potters. He found, too, a number of Wesleyan day-schools, many of them under the charge of his grandfather's old students, and gave much time to helping them in such ways as he could in their devoted but often frustrating work. While he was there the *Life of Charles Kingsley* was published, and it was perhaps that book, and the shocking lack of any principles of hygiene and sanitation, of which he was even then having personal experience in the community around him, which first attracted him to Christian Socialism and brought to him the realization of the scarcity of enlightened men and women prepared to help in educating the people to their needs.

Education in those days was still a narrow affair of 'school business', centring in the Primary Schools especially on the three R's, expressive of that Nonconformist narrow-mindedness which Matthew Arnold so deplored. The young Wesleyan minister deplored it too as he went out of his way in his first circuit to see the practical work of his grandfather's old students. Perhaps with memories of his experiences when, still in his early teens, he had been a district visitor in the riverside slums of East Greenwich, he organized concerts for the old folk at the local Workhouse. Even at that early period of his life he was alert to new avenues of approach to people and new methods by which people might broaden and deepen their minds.

He never grew out of that inquiring, experimental turn of mind, as is evidenced in his genuine interest in, for example, visual aids to education. For it was at the age of ninety-seven that he wrote an article for the official journal of the National

Committee for Visual Aids in Education in which he spoke of the motor-car and the film as two great instruments which had helped to promote and enrich the experience and the enjoyment of natural wonders. It would have been natural in a man of his age in 1952 merely to applaud such new aids to education, or bitterly to attack them. Characteristically he accepted the new scientific methods, but at the same time sounded a note of warning: pictures, aids of that sort, must be used to inspire and enrich the imagination, not stultify it—a warning badly needed today. 'The watchword therefore of films in education shall be the promotion, not of the abstract truth, but of its full meaning in "the truth, the whole truth, and nothing but the truth", and this by ministering to the imagination of the scholar in aid of his understanding.'

When Scott Lidgett went from Tunstall to Southport, one can well believe that it was as a relief from its stiff respectability, rather than as an onerous duty, that he spent five to seven hours each day in reading and study, for that was his self-inflicted task in these formative years. During his three years in Southport he studied in the privacy of his own room, he conducted Bible Classes for the somewhat inhibited Young Gentlemen and Young Ladies of the private schools with which the town abounded, he made new friends, and most important of all, he developed still more his friendship with Dr W. B. Pope, who had just finished his year of office as President of the Wesleyan Methodist Conference. He was never to forget the conversation with him in which the ex-President related his triumph in persuading the Conference to accept 'Our Father' as the definition of God in the Catechism.[4]

In that conversation another seed was sown in the mind of John Scott Lidgett. It was to strike roots and flower not only in theology, but in practical education. It began to grow rapidly when, after the normal three-year period at Southport, Scott Lidgett moved to Cardiff. At Tunstall he had been shocked by the mental poverty of people because helpers were so few; at Southport he had felt frustrated by the mental poverty resulting from too much wealth and poor use of leisure

[4] See p. 84, *supra*.

time; in Cardiff he was to find commerce hand-in-hand with social progress, minds alert to experiences and vision, people prepared to serve their fellows and to take decisive steps toward their God. It was a fortunate coincidence that it was during his three years in Cardiff that the *Life of Frederick Denison Maurice* was published.[5]

The spur of Christian Socialism touched him the more realistically because of the experiences of circuit life in the previous six years, for he was able to consider the work of nineteenth-century philanthropy critically. He saw that too much of the work of the earlier evangelicals was little more than a superficial remedy of obvious defects in social structure, 'palliative rather than reconstructive', as he himself has described it. At a later stage of his life, Scott Lidgett was fond of using Keats's description of the world as 'a vale of soul-making', but however conscious he was of that, however much his eyes were set on the mountain of the Lord, he took good care to keep his own feet on the ground and his mind and heart geared to his feet. He added to the slogans of the Methodist 'Forward Movement', 'God cares not only for souls but for bodies', his profound conviction that God cares also for minds. But he never forgot that, whether one was dealing with bodies or with minds, it was the spirit that inspired and co-ordinated all successful effort.

Cardiff was another step in the stairway which took Scott Lidgett up to the road along which he was to guide young and old in a life of service, for there he found opportunities of putting into practice theories already formulated, and fellow-workers of like aspirations prepared to translate theories into sheer hard work. He organized youth not only to preach the Gospel, but to illustrate it by showing healthy ways of occupying leisure time—and in a dockside city like Cardiff there were plenty of opportunities for the unhealthy filling of leisure time. Concert parties and choirs were organized, especially to safeguard the moral welfare of young soldiers stationed near the city; a new church was built by his efforts in a working-class

---

[5] For his own view of F. D. Maurice, see his *Idea of God and Social Ideals*, pp. 92-5, 102, cf. pp. 99f., *supra*.

district; with the all too blatant examples of intemperance in plain view, he strengthened the temperance movement in the city; and he took great interest in the Mission to Seamen down in the dock area.

At Cardiff, indeed, the experiences he had known amongst working-class folk in the Potteries were continued, and his methods of serving the more unfortunate were extended, but it was also in Cardiff that he came into direct contact with a side of education which in the last sixty years of his life he never left—the University. He arrived in Cardiff when the movement to found a University College of South Wales was reaching its climax. What influence his experiences of those days had on his future work in education cannot be estimated, but it was certainly a happy chance (he himself would have described it as another example of the 'guided life' in which he so strongly believed), and a tribute to his intellectual stature, that at the age of twenty-seven, deeply read, his mind already disciplined and sensitive to the needs of his day, he was able to exchange views with such men as the Rev. Dr Charles J. Vaughan, then Dean of Llandaff and Master of the Temple, with the first Principal of the infant University College, Dr J. Viriamu Jones, F.R.S., an old fellow-student of his at University College, London, with Professor Andrew Seth Pringle-Pattison, with Professor W. P. Ker, with Professor T. R. Roberts, then a disciple of Hegel. Young as he was, his intellectual stature was recognized by these men, and Scott Lidgett was a member of the Committee which in 1883 founded the new University College in Cardiff and one of the members of the first University College Court. Just as he had experienced the painful contrast of the over-poor and the over-fed in his first two circuits, so in Cardiff in the one city he saw equally painful contrasts— between the degradation and the squalor of a seaport and the fine intellectual and spiritual strivings of a potential University.

Another contrast awaited him at Wolverhampton, his next circuit, to which he went as a married man. For purposes of this essay there is no need to dwell on the part that this circuit played in formulating his view of education save to mention one point: it was there that he developed further what he had done in all his circuits, often with the far from veiled disapproval of fellow ministers—the organization of leisure-time pursuits.

This theme he was to develop yet more fully in his work at the Bermondsey Settlement and on the London School Board. It is interesting to recall a brush he later had with Dr Dinsdale T. Young on this matter. In 1896, at the Liverpool Conference, the Rev. C. H. Kelly presented his report on the Committee for the Youth of Methodism and the Rev. W. D. FitzGerald tried to obtain stronger official backing for the Wesley Guild of which he was General Secretary. A debate, fanned by the Rev. Hugh Price Hughes, sprang up, and the Rev. Dinsdale T. Young championed the official view of what were still considered by many Methodist (and other) worthies as distractions, and rashly stated: 'In Wales, Mr President, we do not need recreation!' With memories of what he had seen in the Potteries, on the South Wales quaysides and Wolverhampton, and with the experience of what little had been done to support him officially, Scott Lidgett unexpectedly rose to champion the Youth Committee. 'The sooner we recognize that recreation unorganized is a danger, the better', he said. 'Some of us have seen poor and ignorant factory girls called to God first by giving them healthy physical recreation.' His speech carried Conference, and the Wesley Guild thenceforward for many years formed the spearhead of organized Christian use of leisure time. At the time of that Liverpool Conference, Scott Lidgett had already founded the Bermondsey Settlement, which after six years of hard struggle was thus beginning to show forth fruits from the seeds that he had sown.

It was Cambridge, however, that brought to a climax the formative influence which had been steadily turning Scott Lidgett into the path of education, and it was owing to the personal interest of the Rev. Dr W. F. Moulton that he was appointed there at the age of thirty-three. Methodism was not strong then in that University city, and one of the first things the new minister did was to organize leisure-time interests for the boys of the town. His own chief interests, naturally enough, were focused on the dons and undergraduates, but his concern was spread over a much wider field. Here Scott Lidgett can best speak for himself: 'I had become deeply concerned about the growing separation, and the consequent estrangement, of the different social classes, which led not only to political and economic strife, but to a class-consciousness and self-enclosed narrowness which was as gravely injurious to the more prosperous class, to say the least of it, as it was to those whom they employed. I had determined that my lot must be cast with the heathen and that whatever influences I might gain should be devoted to creating relationships of "sharing" between all classes, and of personal service, extending beyond the limits of the ordinary Church work to embrace all the interests of the community, on the part of the well-to-do, educated, and leisured.'[6]

His own experiences, outlined above, brought him to these conclusions, but having reached them he came more and more to realize that his grandfather, John Scott, had reached them though in a different age and by a different path, many years before. From this time onward to the end of his life he was profoundly conscious of his grandfather's influence, and from his Address on 'The Working Classes entitled to a Good Education' he quoted more frequently than from any other book except the Bible. As his secretary mentions: 'The Address very rarely left his side.' The fact that in a comparatively short book, published in 1936, Scott Lidgett himself spent three pages in giving a summary of the Address, speaks for itself.[7] John Scott had a clear, logical mind; so had Scott Lidgett. John Scott was a fighter, not afraid of letting his mind be known even when he was in a minority of one; the same was true of Scott Lidgett. There was a humanity and broad-mindedness about John Scott which was noticeably absent from Nonconformists of his day; and this trait too is seen in the grandson. One point in John Scott's Address must be specially stressed, for it was the very point that Scott Lidgett found it necessary to stress in his own lifetime. Speaking to the students of Westminster College, John Scott had said: 'You, however, will never forget that it is with *mind* that you have to deal—that it is *mind* which you have to draw out, and mould, and fit for its duties to itself, to

[6] *My Guided Life*, pp. 59-60.   [7] ibid., pp. 12-15.

mankind and to its Maker. From the child's first entrance into your school, your object is to train him to *think*, and to teach him *how* to think. All that you tell him in your lessons, and all that he reads in his lesson-books, are to supply him with material for thought; then the school process, step by step, is to instruct him how to use those materials.' The influence of the first Principal of Westminster College on the mind and heart of the grandson cannot be over-estimated, as Scott Lidgett was never to forget. He said of his grandfather: 'I have tried to carry on the spiritual and educational work of which he was a striking and influential example.'

A good deal of space has been given to the formative experiences of Scott Lidgett's first thirty-three years. But it is necessary, for by the time he reached that age his view of education was shaped. It derived directly from the concept of the Fatherhood of God and its logical corollary, the brotherhood of man. In his fourteen years as a circuit minister, Scott Lidgett had come to abhor the estrangement between the social classes, and to work for the 'underdog', but he came to know that that work could only be effective through education. 'From the outset of my career', he wrote, 'my main concern had been theological. So far from my educational and other social activities having been a departure from this concern, they have been entirely based upon my construction of what is involved in the Christian revelation of God and particularly in His Fatherhood.' But he found gradually that he could not recognize the Sovereign Personality of God without stressing both in theory and practice the importance of man's personality and the need for decisive steps to develop it. 'Christian ethics, if their principles be fully embraced and their essential presuppositions be accepted, are the only means of social safety, stability, and progress. They are so deeply founded in reason and reality that, instead of ossifying past traditions, they call men to the adventurous reflections that will guide and stimulate courageous endeavours to transform our imperfect and unsatisfactory civilization in their light.'[8] These views he expressed in diverse forms in speech and in print. Nowhere are they better brought

[8] *God and the World*, p. 71.

into focus than in his collection of essays (dedicated to the memory of the Rev. Dr W. B. Pope) entitled *God and the World*.

Eleven years after his call to the Christian Ministry he answered an equally decisive call—to education. During those eleven years, through his own energetic probing into social problems, he had had more practical experience of education and of social pioneering than falls to the lot of the average minister. He had learned much of the economic difficulties of people in strikingly different parts of the country. He had come to know the 'privileged and the unprivileged' (a phrase he himself was fond of using), and by the time he went to Cambridge in 1887 he knew that his future work would lie largely in the removal of what the word 'unprivileged' represented. Others shared his view, but in his own Church none appreciated the view from such a clear intellectual angle. He was conscious of that, and therefore on occasions found himself out of sympathy with his own Church because he felt it did not concern itself sufficiently with the need for mental as well as physical advance if a real spiritual awakening was to be achieved. 'I could not be content with appeals that sought rather to palliate existing evils by charitable help than radically to reconstruct the existing organization of society on the basis of righteousness—the comradeship of brotherly love.'

Contact with dons and undergraduates at Cambridge only strengthened and brought this view into sharper focus. He spent Sunday evenings after service with men who not only had intellectual gifts but used them; he spent Monday evenings with those same men in conversation on spiritual matters. Neither he nor they were to forget those hours of fellowship. 'So in all these ways', he writes, 'the train was laid and only the spark was needed to kindle the flame. It came about as follows. On the last Sunday evening in November 1887 Temperance Sunday was observed as usual, and on the evening of that day I preached a sermon at Hills Road Wesleyan Church to a large congregation, partly composed of boys of The Leys School, which at that time had no chapel of its own, and with a fair sprinkling of undergraduates. My text was, "And whether one member suffereth, all the members suffer with it" (1 Corinthians 12²⁶). Deeply moved by my subject, I endeavoured to describe the spiritual, intellectual, and physical conditions which did so much to strengthen the temptations to intemperance in crowded cities, and dealt, in a way that has since become familiar, with the wholeness of society, and with the spiritual loss sustained by the well-to-do, educated, and leisured from their failure to share their advantages and to co-operate with the industrial classes in remedying these adverse and demoralizing conditions. On the following day I learned from many sources of the deep impression my sermon had made upon the congregation, and especially upon the masters and boys of The Leys School. During that week I heard what seemed to be a clear and imperative call from God. It cost me a great effort to give up finally, as it seemed to me, my theological and philosophical ambitions. But I could not hold out, and on the Thursday night of that week, as I was returning from conducting a service at the little village of Quy, I stood under a moonlit but stormy sky and vowed to God that I would renounce all other interests, and seek to lead a movement to give practical and permanent expression to the sympathy my sermon had been the means of evoking.'[9]

So began the Bermondsey Settlement about which another writes in this book. One point, however, must be mentioned here. When recalling those days from the vantage point of 1950, Scott Lidgett tells how he sought out the most neglected parts of poor London, and how, after receiving advice on all hands, he and his fellows found just the utterly neglected, squalid spot he wanted—in Bermondsey. Did he in that time of exploration live again the experience of his grandfather, John Scott, who when he had at last persuaded the Methodist Connexion of the need for a training-college for teachers, searched the London of 1846-7 for a site where uncared-for children were most numerous and the need therefore greatest? We cannot doubt it. In answering this second call to education, Scott Lidgett renounced all that he had been most interested in, but, he says, 'the remarkable thing was that, in serving Bermondsey, God

[9] *My Guided Life*, p. 63.

gave me back in fuller measure all I had renounced and enabled me to do theological and educational and social work—the University classes, the county councils and the rest—and to carry out all that I had thought I should have for ever to relinquish'.

Although Scott Lidgett welcomed interest and help from members of all denominations in the Universities, he received special encouragement, as he himself has recorded, from the Wesley Societies at Oxford, Cambridge, Edinburgh, and Aberystwyth, and he went out of his way to interest the Methodist boarding-schools in his project. He visited or corresponded with Kingswood, Wesley College, Sheffield, Queen's College, Taunton, Launceston College, Woodhouse Grove, Laleham, Kent College, Canterbury, the East Anglian School, Bury St Edmunds (now Culford), Congleton, Rydal Mount (now Rydal), Lytham, and Craigmore College. All these, in some way or another, were associated with the early years of the Bermondsey Settlement. An annual meeting was held at each school at which a collection was taken to help the scheme financially, and to awaken the interest of pupils, especially those who might be going later to live in London and who could serve at the Settlement in some capacity. Letters were sent by Scott Lidgett to School Magazines, for he felt it important to go out of his way to stimulate an interest in a work which would have been very near to the heart of John Wesley himself. 'We are trying to proclaim the need and duty of a larger spirit of social service, and of a more brotherly fellowship of rich with poor, than London at present manifests, and we are assured that until that spirit is more fully present the Kingdom of God cannot be greatly advanced.'

His view of education had been sharpened to the point of a goad which drove him into the practical working out of the sacred principle laid down earlier by his grandfather: 'That as good an education should be given to the poor as their children can receive.' The difficulties of the work were not unrealized. He recognized with pain—and was to do so even more as the work progressed—that true education had often been hindered by the Church, that it had been neglected by the State, opposed by the well-to-do, and not demanded by the poor themselves. It would be wrong to say that at the age of thirty-three his view of education had been finally shaped, for to the day of his death Scott Lidgett's mind was open to the stimulus of new ideas, new challenges, new methods; but from the time he left Cambridge and circuit work for Bermondsey and the slums, education was for him a constant challenge, demanding work, prayer, battle for a more widespread realization that all men, privileged and unprivileged, belong to one another, and that all belong to God the Father. How modern sound the words he spoke to the students of Westminster College in 1909: 'In an age impatient of external restraints and seeking enjoyment often of a frivolous and selfish kind, we cannot too persistently endeavour to set duty before the eyes of children, alike in the sternness of her authority and the benignancy of her grace. But duty must have content, must direct, conduct and desire to an end. What is this to be? The first answer is that we all belong to a great community, and that the ideal of life is the sense of membership of that community, and the desire to render service to it.'

Thenceforth, therefore, Scott Lidgett worked for the development of mind, body, and spirit in community life: the development of a balanced personality. But what he sought to achieve for others through fellowship with each other, he himself had to achieve through loneliness. There were many fellow ministers in the 1890s who looked askance at his radical views; there were others later who suspected and feared what might more truly be called his ecumenical views. All this left him quite undisturbed. In fact we cannot help suspecting that he enjoyed a fight, and always, even in his earliest days, he was a formidable opponent. He had the fortunate knack of always being able to judge a situation—and then make the best of it. But it would be wrong to think that he was entirely a happy man. He was human, he had his little conceits and foibles (which became more noticeable as he grew older), he had no personal magnetism, and he was lonely, for he was—as most great men are—a man of passion, without which he could not have exhibited the insight and tremendous zest for life that was his.

Only once did he hesitate, and it was his loyalty to his own denomination and to his ministerial vocation which made him do so. When he started work in Bermondsey he deliberately set social rather than ecclesiastical duties in the foreground. He canvassed the intelligentsia of the University of Cambridge; he visited the Methodist boarding-schools and tried to stimulate their social conscience; he startled local Methodist worthies at a Leicester church (one would like to have been present) by opening an address with the announcement that he was the proprietor of a billiard saloon and a licensed retailer of tobacco. He had no doubts about the ultimate object and therefore no qualms about the methods he was adopting—until inevitably he came up against politics. There lay the point of hesitation.

With all his deep intellectualism, Scott Lidgett was a practical man. Mere preaching on the theme of the Fatherhood of God and the Brotherhood of man was not going to improve the lot of those he had determined to help, and only in rare cases would it win recruits to help him in his work. G. B. Shaw at that time was still a voice crying in the wilderness. His was not the only voice, but the others also were still voices only. Scott Lidgett preferred the picture of a man working in the slums, and that meant getting amongst the people, and not merely preaching from pulpits, speaking on platforms, or writing for publication. Inevitably, therefore, he quickly found himself in the net of politics, and it was not long after he had started to make his home and his work in Bermondsey that he was approached by the local Progressive Party to become a candidate in the election of Poor Law Guardians. He had no doubt about what his course of action ought to be, but he recognized the danger, and probably more forcibly than ever before, he realized a conflict of loyalties. He consulted the man who had been largely responsible for the trust which Conference had placed in him in allowing him to go to Bermondsey, the Rev. Dr W. F. Moulton, and pointed out the risks which might attend his becoming involved in the civic side of affairs in Bermondsey, and therefore in political wrangling. Looking the young Warden straight in the face with a solemnity which Scott Lidgett never forgot, Dr Moulton replied: 'Mr Lidgett, we sent you to South London to take risks.' From that time onwards Scott Lidgett never hesitated to take them. There is, after all, a sense in which every man whose life and personality are in any way significant transcends the bounds of social class, political party and religious denomination. So it proved in this case.

Scott Lidgett's greatest testing time as far as educational affairs were concerned came at the turn of the century, in the events which led up to and followed the passing of the Education Act of 1902. Up to that time it may be said that Scott Lidgett was learning, practically as well as theoretically, and was experimenting; from that time onward he continued to experiment, though with a surer hand, and he was beginning to take a leading part in educational affairs, his influence spreading far beyond the confines of his own Church, largely because of the statesmanlike manner in which he had handled extreme difficulties.

To one who has studied the man and the educational problems of that time, Scott Lidgett's position is puzzling, and the clue can only be found in a close study of his own educational practice at Bermondsey and of the complexities of the growing State-cum-Church interest in national education. In one of his Reports he wrote that the Settlement was 'an honest attempt to make Christian work more civic, and civic work more Christian, in sympathy and aim. In both those endeavours we are at one with all that is most enlightened and far-seeing in the thought of our times. All well-informed Christians are coming to recognize that ministry to the spiritual interests of men involves care and effort for all that belongs to them; that the well-being of the individual can only be secured by that of the community; and that the most practical demand made upon Christian faith is that it should leaven and transform the State. And, approaching the subject from the other side, the educational, administrative, and social interests of the community—a truly Christian concern—will be served best by the high aims and general disinterestedness of truly Christian men, who have the courage to carry out sometimes disagreeable tasks, and the patience and fidelity which a time-serving and men-pleasing spirit can never inspire.'

In those years Scott Lidgett had his full share of the 'disagreeable tasks'. But before tracing his own part in educational developments, one ought to recall the background as it existed in 1896, when it had become manifest to anyone who had close dealings with education—and Scott Lidgett had come very close to it indeed at Bermondsey—that matters could not long continue as they were.

The old bad system of 'payment by results' against which grandfather John Scott had inveighed with such weighty vehemence had come to an end in 1870, when W. E. Forster, after a thirty-day debate and with the active support of his Prime Minister, had at last succeeded in forcing his Education Bill through Parliament. However much that Bill may be criticized and regarded as a mere compromise, it did at least mark the end of *laissez-faire* in the provision of education. Henceforth the State was committed. Major problems had come to the fore in the minds of all thinking men and women: Should denominational schools receive public money in their support? Should school attendance, at least in the primary stage, be compulsory? If so, should children be compelled to attend schools provided by a religious denomination other than their own? Since by that time all denominations had recognized the essential place of religion in education, battles were already raging round the place of religious instruction in the schools, and each denomination was preparing hotly to defend its own interests. These matters had already caused many of the difficulties in the passage of the Forster Act, and a Mr Cowper-Temple had proposed the insertion of a clause which has both helped and hindered ever since: that 'no religious catechism or religious formulary distinctive of any particular denomination shall be taught in the (board) school'. As Professor Lester Smith has written: 'The compromise succeeded in leashing the dogs of controversy without preventing religious education.'

Scott Lidgett was only a youth of sixteen when the Forster Act was passed. His work at the Bermondsey Settlement brought him into intimate touch, not with petty sectarian prejudices, but with the major problem of providing education for the hordes of children and young people in East London; it revealed the equally urgent problem of persuading those children and their parents that education was needed, but the problem of what denomination should supply it did not present any great difficulty to him personally. As we have seen already, he was strongly influenced, too, by the views and the decisive actions of his grandfather, who was a true Wesleyan Methodist in that he had never set bounds to the scope of education.

In 1896 the Bryce Commission had just made its nine-volume Report on Secondary Education. Its recommendations may be briefly summarized as the setting-up of a Ministry of Education, assisted by an advisory body of persons conversant with education and holding an independent position; the compilation and maintenance of a register of teachers; and the decentralization of administration by the establishment of local education authorities in counties and county boroughs. Scott Lidgett, with his interest in developing minds, could not but sympathize with these recommendations. In that same year he had been appointed secretary of the special committee set up by Wesleyan Methodism to consider what proved to be the unsuccessful forerunner of the 1902 Education Act, and at once he was faced with problems different from those he was tackling so successfully at the Settlement. In primary education the voluntary schools established by various denominations were finding it impossible to collect sufficient money to maintain them at the level of the rate-aided Board-schools set up as a result of the Forster Act. As Dr A. W. Harrison has written of Wesleyan educational policy, 'We were never whole-hearted believers in denominational education', and by 1890 it had become official Wesleyan policy to encourage School Boards everywhere and to see that a Christian non-sectarian school should be placed within reach of every family. That could only be accomplished by the State.

The difficulties arose over the methods the State proposed. A Bill was framed by Sir John Gorst, Vice-President of the Education Department, which found favour with no one. The Wesleyan Education Committee, of which Scott Lidgett was a member, objected to it because it gave additional financial help to schools without accompanying it by adequate and representative management, so that those denominations wealthy enough to provide many schools would be given still greater powers over those denominations which had not. Scott Lidgett duly recorded the protests of his Wesleyan Methodist committee, but characteristically he began to delve into the pros and cons of the whole business. It was during this period that he came to have close personal contact with Sir John Gorst (the man who, incidentally, 'saw no difficulties' in overcoming opposition to rate-aid for voluntary schools), and one cannot but assume that he came also to have some inkling of the unorthodox happenings which were beginning to take place in the Education Department, and which led to the emergence of Robert Morant as the greatest educational planner of his generation. It would be interesting to know whether he had any close personal contact with that gentleman too. Opposition to the proposed Bill of 1890 came from all sides, and it was withdrawn, but it had served to demonstrate that no political party dare disregard the growing concern and tension over educational matters.

Within his own denomination, too, he came to realize the strong pull of opposing forces, though in those very conflicts of opinion there is at least evidence of the life and idealism which were stirring in no uncertain manner. On the one hand he found himself listening to the deeply entrenched conservatism of the Rev. Dr J. H. Rigg (who had followed his grandfather as Principal of Westminster College), and finding therein much to digest and respect; on the other hand, the liberal views of the Rev. Hugh Price Hughes also found a responsive chord, though Scott Lidgett never felt quite at ease with the Welsh enthusiasm of the great Nonconformist leader.

As has already been indicated, his interest in the thought and work of Frederick Denison Maurice was focused at just the crucial point of his own development. In particular, he found in Maurice's philosophy the guidance he needed in unifying the various aspects of thought and experience which were becoming peculiarly his own—denominational, ecclesiastical, educational, spiritual, secular, and, before long, national. In those closing years of the nineteenth century it was the practical implications of Maurice's philosophy which chiefly attracted Scott Lidgett, for he was able to work them out in his own experience in London. His election to the London School Board in 1897 as member for the Southwark Division (a position he held till the Board gave place to the London County Council in 1903), gave him that opportunity on a wider plane than had so far been possible in the Settlement. He felt that his election was a victory for the cause of education, for social and Christian principles, a demonstration of the position which the Settlement had come to hold in local confidence. 'The work is exacting', he wrote, 'for it takes me an average of twenty hours each week to discharge the duties with fair efficiency, but the greatness of the issues involved is worth almost any sacrifice of time and strength.'

Determined as he was to train minds, he did not make the mistake often made by intellectuals of neglecting hobbies and what one might call the manual and practical leisure-time occupations, and of believing that the study of books was the only approach to mental development. Under the London School Board, for example, lessons were encouraged in cookery, woodwork, and metalwork (the first centre having been started in 1885 by a London teacher), clay modelling, painting, paper-folding, drawing. It was also the London School Board that had led the way in the encouragement of games—football, cricket and swimming in particular. Such matters are taken for granted today; they were the subject of ribald and destructive criticism in the 1890s. The Warden of the Bermondsey Settlement was coming to know their true value.

The sheer volume of work that Scott Lidgett accomplished during those years is reason for wonder, but during it all, his keen, analytical mind was sifting, absorbing, registering, qualifying, until as the educational and denominational struggle came to a head he was able, if not to see his way clearly, at least to steer with a sure judgement. His view of English education by the close of the nineteenth century may be thus summarized:

(*a*) State interest in secondary education was long overdue, and in thinking this he was wholly in agreement with Dr J. H. Rigg. Untidy as he was in person, he hated muddle in administration, and any measure that sought to remedy the muddle revealed by the Bryce Commission would have his personal support. The 'Cockerton Judgement' probably annoyed him considerably, with its interference with the sound work for a more advanced education that his own Board was undertaking, especially as he was one of the three members of the London School Board most responsible for higher education at that time, but (although he has left no record of his thoughts) he was certainly perspicacious enough to realize that ultimately the very spotlight of publicity thus provided would lead inevitably to greater illumination and to a more realistic recognition of the needs of higher education.

(b) Although the School Boards in some areas, notably his own, had been valiantly experimenting and meeting with no small measure of success, yet all lacked 'drive' and all were in danger of being stifled by vested interests.

(c) The Churches which hitherto had helped education at all levels through their voluntary schools possessed the 'drive' which the School Boards lacked, but had no financial resources to carry out good intentions.

(d) A better supply of trained and educated teachers was becoming increasingly needed.

(e) Clashes between State authority (whether central or delegated) and the Churches were regrettably inevitable, especially in the matter of provision and maintenance of schools and in that of religious instruction.

These were not the merely academic views of a highly intellectual clergyman; they were the convictions of a man in actual touch with girls and boys, young men and women, the privileged and the unprivileged, in what was now his home in Bermondsey; they were the convictions of a man who was himself engaged in the 'rough and tumble' of party politics; they were the outcome of experience as a member of the School Board which more than any other School Board was blazing a trail for others to follow later. Space forbids quotation here, but his own all too brief account of the work undertaken during those years by the London School Board should be read.[10]

The clash which Scott Lidgett had realized was inevitable came in 1902 when Sir Robert Morant engineered a new Education Bill. This, briefly, proposed to abolish the School Boards and to substitute local education authorities, which should take over the control of voluntary and former Board-schools (as far as secular instruction was concerned) and give them rate aid, though the managers of these 'non-provided' schools were to continue to be responsible for religious instruction, in connexion with which the Cowper-Temple clause was to be retained (hence the term: 'the Dual System'). At the same time, the new Local Education Authorities were empowered to provide secondary and higher education (which included the setting-up of training colleges).

At once the storm broke, and in Nonconformity its thunder has re-echoed ever since. Scott Lidgett was a member of the education committee of a denomination whose views were sharply divided on the merits of the proposed Bill; he had only recently been elected Secretary of the National Free Church Council Education Committee, which was pledged to support the extension of the School Board system and to champion the allegedly slighted Nonconformists; and yet all his own experience and educational beliefs tended to support the increased opportunities that the Bill seemed to offer. He was in a most difficult position and knew it. It is not without significance that it was at this point in his career that he began to turn increasingly to the Addresses which his grandfather had delivered to the students of Westminster College, and that he realized to the full that the views expressed were as applicable to the needs of his own day as they had been to the needs of the 1860s—a fact which is scarcely complimentary to educational progress. 'As long as the Wesleyans pretend to give education to the poor, they will give them an education which it will be worth their while to receive and to pay for as far as they are able', John Scott had said. Surely, as the Warden of the Bermondsey Settlement moved among the pioneers of what

[10] *My Guided Life*, pp. 172-6.

was soon to be the London County Council, as he talked with men in Whitehall at the Department of Education (soon to be called the Board of Education), as always at the end of the day he turned once more to the east end with all its squalor and all its potentiality, he must have experienced a more than whimsical kinship with his illustrious relative who had fought against the evils of 'payment by results', who had been the confidant of Matthew Arnold, who had talked on even terms with the great men of Whitehall, and who had returned in the evening to the squalor of Strutton Ground.

It was the question of the School Boards that worried him most. He knew, probably better than any Methodist minister, the evils inherent in the vested interests in which some School Boards were enmeshed, but he knew too the fine pioneer work that his own School Board was doing—work which he would have thought possible in every School Board in the country. His own Church was pledged to support the spread of the School Board system, though his own inquiries in educational circles had already revealed the necessity for firm and probably drastic action by the State, if the education of the country was to keep pace with national achievements in other spheres and if it was to continue to compete successfully with other countries whose intellectual enlightenment had been steadily overhauling Britain's. He himself had pioneered an educational experiment whereby education was made more easily available for folk to whom it had previously been denied—the very thing that some parts of the proposed Bill were designed to do. In fact he was in full agreement with the view expressed in the *Daily Mail* by Sidney Webb: 'For the first time the Bill definitely includes as a public function education as education, not primary education only, or technical education only, but anything and everything that is education from the Kindergarten to the University. This renders the Bill of 1902 epoch-making in the history of English education.' Another factor possibly influenced Scott Lidgett: at quite an early stage in the Bill's history, party political manœuvring took a hand. Lloyd George saw in the Bill a heaven-sent opportunity to re-unite the Liberal party. Scott Lidgett with his practical experience and his contacts at the Board of Education was sensitive and critical of anything savouring of something no higher than political strategy.

There was another Methodist of the day who shared Scott Lidgett's divided views on the merits and demerits of the Bill—the Rev. Hugh Price Hughes. He too appreciated the bewildering tangle of educational administration; he too recognized the inevitable conflicts of loyalty which all sections of the Church would have to meet; he too recognized the sheer cleverness of the somewhat Machiavellian figure who had pushed forward the Bill—Sir Robert Morant. Both men realized that only one solution was possible—compromise. Both were courageous enough to say so. Each of them stood, or rather thought, above the narrowing limits of mere denominationalism. Death was very near to Hugh Price Hughes and his share in those troubled years is largely forgotten; Scott Lidgett's career was but half run and his share came to be remembered—and to be suspected, the more so as he extended his work more and more for the closer union of the Protestant Churches. In 1902 Hughes and Lidgett stood together, but Hughes was the leader; it was only the sudden shock of the latter's death that made Scott Lidgett realize that henceforth in this matter of education he had to be the leader.

Nevertheless, whatever might be Scott Lidgett's view in private, in public he spoke vehemently against certain clauses of the Bill, ranging himself against Dr J. H. Rigg, who, incidentally, has never been given the credit that is rightly his for his lifelong advocacy of State help for higher education. At a specially convened meeting of the Wesleyan Methodist Education Committee, Scott Lidgett, with his thought centred especially on the Board of which he was a leading member, pointed to the proven usefulness and democratic principle of the School Boards, and doubted whether the proposed local education authorities could ever become such satisfactory instruments of control. His voice eventually carried official Methodism, but opinion was sharply divided—and understandably. After all, it was not only the Roman Catholics and Anglicans who had founded schools; Wesleyan Methodism still owned a large number, and just as urgently needed the financial help proffered by the Bill. A great meeting was held in St James Hall, London, to protest against the Bill's iniquities. Grievances were undeniable. As G. A. N. Lowndes has summarized the position in his *Silent Social Revolution* Nonconformists could claim 'that in 12,000 out of 14,000 denominational schools conducted by and in the interests of a single denomination, 8,000 to 9,500 of them being the only schools available in the district, 700,000 Methodist and perhaps 300,000 other Nonconformist children were either being compelled to make themselves conspicuous by withdrawal from religious instruction or to run the risk of petty proselytization. They could add that so far from seeking to end this injustice the Government were proposing to perpetuate it by compelling the parents to support it out of the rates, thus incidentally relieving the squire, the parson, and the richer inhabitants of the parish from the burden of its support. Moreover, they could show that although the Government could not produce a single precedent where ratepayers had not a controlling voice in the management of a fund derived from the rates, the proposals in the Bill would ensure that the two representative managers appointed by the Local Authority would be in a permanent minority. Worse still, in any one of these 14,000 schools no head teacher could be a Nonconformist and few Nonconformist children could hope to become pupil teachers without accepting Anglican Baptism.'[11]

The outcome of that meeting in St James Hall was unanimous and uncompromising opposition to the Bill. The Principal of Mansfield College, Dr A. M. Fairbairn, led a deputation to the Prime Minister to tell him so. The Rev. Dr John Clifford assumed the leadership of revolt and during the summer of 1902 organized a Passive Resistance Movement whose adherents pledged themselves to refuse to pay rates.

Scott Lidgett was present at the mass meeting, he was a member of the deputation that waited on the Prime Minister, but he was not a convinced supporter. As he himself has written: 'Both my antecedents and my sympathies... prevented me from adopting the extreme hostility to the denominational

[11] op. cit., pp. 84-5. See also *Hansard*, Vol. CVII.

schools which prevailed, for the most part, in the Nonconformist opposition.' He was sincere enough in his opposition to these clauses of the Bill which seemed unjust to Nonconformists, but at the same time he took steps to ensure that those he served (notably the Free Church Council) did not take the extreme measures of revolt from which he foresaw there could be no honourable withdrawal. Again to quote his own words: 'During the autumn of 1902, I was busily engaged upon the subject [educational controversy] and particularly in a successful endeavour to keep the National Free Church Council from identifying itself with the Passive Resistance Movement.'

Despite Nonconformist and Liberal opposition, despite one of the most bitterly contested passages in Parliamentary history, the Education Bill of 1902 passed into law. The five years or so which followed must have tested the physical, mental, and spiritual strength of the man as did no other period in his life. In all matters bearing on social reform or education (and there was plenty of activity during those years), with no obvious effort on his part but simply by wise statesmanship in a time of deep-seated resentment, Scott Lidgett had become the acknowledged leader of orthodox Nonconformity—if one can so term the more moderate majority. A reading of the other essays in this book will make it clear that during this period, as throughout his life, Scott Lidgett never neglected his duties as a preacher, never laid on one side his theological scholarship, never let his 'drive' slacken in the constructive work of the Bermondsey Settlement. Yet educational matters alone were of sufficient number and sufficient importance to have provided the average man with a full-time job. So one can judge the stature of Scott Lidgett.

He was by this time a leader of the London School Board. He had served, or was serving, on the General Purposes Committee of that Board; he was Vice-Chairman of the School Management Committee (which superintended nearly the whole of the educational work), Chairman of the special Sub-Committee charged with the management of the higher elementary and higher grade schools of London, with the teaching of Science and Art, with Manual Instruction and method in Infant Schools; he was a member of the Committee which dealt with special schools for the blind, deaf, and defective; he was on the Teaching Staff Sub-Committee of higher standard schools and on the managing committee of the Brentwood Industrial Schools. Like other leading members of the London School Board he was seriously concerned about the future, for the 1902 Education Act had given very wide powers to Borough Councils, and it had become obvious that much of the good that had been done for the education of London Children would be undone unless there was to be some cohesion between the various Borough Councils in the metropolitan area, involving as it did the control of 2,000 institutions, over 20,000 teachers, a million children and students, and an annual expenditure of £4,000,000. The only effective way of ensuring this was a separate Parliamentary Bill for London. This was passed in 1903, and the London County Council was given an over-all control. Nevertheless, the passing of this Bill was by no means a natural corollary of the national Act of the year before. Difficulties and problems were acute, as is made abundantly clear in *The History of the London County Council*. Patience, powers of persuasion, clear-sightedness, strength were needed, and Scott Lidgett was well to the fore in supplying and using these qualities.

After all, education is not the narrow matter of reading, writing, and arithmetic it is often loosely considered to be. All its problems are not invested in religious instruction, as the then hot and bitter debates had made many feel, and to no Methodist was this clearer than it was to Scott Lidgett. Just as his interest in all spheres of education—in primary, secondary, technical, and university—has already been stressed, so must also be stressed his realization of the place of environment, association, and of authority, based, not on Parliamentary laws and municipal regulations, but on a sense of spiritual values. Work on the London School Board had convinced him that the ends of education could not be attained in the schools alone, that public interest had to be aroused in problems of nutrition, health, and housing, that mundane matters like plumbing and the pomp of civic dignity were not distinct; that the populace of London needed a glimpse of the sea, of green fields and woods, and that such green belts as still survived in greater London must at all costs be preserved. These were essentials of education, according to Scott Lidgett, and credit must be given to him for fighting for these things and never losing sight of them when others, equally desirous of educational reform, tended to fix their attention solely on educational administration and sectarian squabbles. He was never a popular figure in the accepted sense of the word—not at any rate until he was a very old man who had become a tradition—and in those years he was courageous enough to make himself definitely unpopular in rousing his fellow Methodists, to say nothing of the rest of nonconformity, from the narrow confines of tea-meetings and catechisms.

Another aspect of Scott Lidgett's work for education which came to the fore in those years was his interest in giving women a larger share in the privileges as well as the responsibilities of life. Although 1884 had seen the extension of the franchise to women, it was not till the first World War that men in general recognized the great work and sacrifice which women were not only capable of making but had actually made. The part that Scott Lidgett played in arousing popular opinion on this matter has not been generally recognized, but it is significant that most of the Commissions on which Scott Lidgett served dealt with the social well-being and progress of women. One of the merits of the London School Board lay in the fact that women were members of it with the same responsibilities and powers as men. One of the difficulties of the proposed LCC Education Bill was that this valuable help would no longer be forthcoming, since women were not at that time allowed to be members of the Council. During his years of service on the LCC Scott Lidgett helped to create an educational organization in which old and young, male and female, played their part.

Scott Lidgett did not believe in revolutions. He could be volcanic enough in his own outbursts, but the nervous excitability which he showed on occasions was not typical. Rather did he believe in steady growth and development, and that implied the unspectacular discharge of duties, large and small, by all concerned. Of the steady growth of the London County Council he wrote: 'It is no exaggeration to say that the policy and progress of the Council, in its formative period, were supplied by religious leaders and sustained by religious influences.'[12] He had seen social progress taking shape; he had that detached sense of awareness to realize that it was progress. In London he attributed much of it to Cardinal Manning, Hugh Price Hughes, Benjamin Waugh, W. T. Stead, Samuel A. Barnett. The man he did not recognize as playing a leading part was himself. Elsewhere, too, he recognized the influence of T. H. Green, Henry Scott Holland, Charles Gore, Edmund S. Talbot, Professor James Stuart, John Brown Paton, Josephine Butler, Millicent Fawcett—all of them inspired in one way or another by Frederick Denison Maurice, all deriving their social ideals from their ideas of God. Like himself, all were visionaries but at the same time men and women of affairs. Because of the recognition among such leaders of the place of God in life, purely secular education up to that time had never found favour, and even the bitter controversies which raged round every attempt by the State to interest itself realistically in education did not until much later in the century turn thinking men from the belief that religion and education were inextricably interwoven.

And yet, having said that, we are bound to add that it must have appeared at times in those first years of the century as though all the argument and frustration, all the hopes and disappointments were so much wasted effort, all the more so to one who was compelled to be as self-contained and lonely as Scott Lidgett was. Perhaps here we find a clue to his inaccessibility, his authoritarianism. He worked steadily on for the cause of education in its broadest sense. He had the ear of leading Nonconformists, of successive Presidents of the Board of Education, of three successive Archbishops of Canterbury, but he lacked a really intimate confidant. He had many sparring partners, many whose conversation and comradeship

---

[12] *Idea of God and Social Ideals*, p. 101.

he valued, and in those contacts he must have found further evidence for the belief that 'personality is the supreme fact and should be the supreme consideration of all social service, whether it be of the State or voluntary effort. Personality must be evoked, stimulated, and sustained if social salvation is to be wrought out.' From a distance of fifty years it is possible to feel even thankful for the quarrels, debates and battles between denominations on the subject, not of religious instruction, but of education in general. It was as though the rubble and broken rock of long-established prejudice were being pressed together and stamped down, so that when the time was ripe a solid educational edifice might be built the more firmly. Is it fantastic to see that edifice in the 1944 Education Act? One thing is certain: the various denominations and those sections of the nation that were forced to become vocal in the early years of this century made one clear statement—that English education, unlike that in other countries, would not tolerate an educational system that was purely secular.

It was true that the Liberal party was pledged to undo the enactments of the 1902 Education Act, but to Scott Lidgett with his progressive and broader-than-party-political views there was solid satisfaction and compensation for his own apparently fruitless work of denominational diplomacy in the manner in which the new local education authorities were quietly facing their problems and all the opportunities offered by that Act. The manner in which some of them called in an independent authority (Sir Michael Sadler) to report on the local needs and possibilities is typical of the progressive spirit abroad, and in that fact, at least, Scott Lidgett found reason for hope, even though sectarian differences seemed no nearer solution.

It was owing partly to the effective behind-the-scenes work which Scott Lidgett performed in connexion with the LCC Bill that in 1918 he was elected leader of the Progressive Party on the Council. That belongs to another chapter, and it is mentioned here merely to stress the commanding position which Scott Lidgett was making for himself by his statesmanship—a fact which produced an even more intense period of activity during 1906 and 1907. The Liberals under Sir Henry

Campbell-Bannerman had come into power in January, pledged to set right the alleged wrongs done to the Nonconformists by the 1902 Act. The Liberals had an overwhelming majority, and there were approximately two hundred Nonconformists in the House; yet no one underestimated the problems involved in passing any Bill which attempted at the same time to give the State control of education and to adjust denominational grievances. A sub-committee was set up to draft the Bill, and Mr Lloyd George was given the task of conferring with Nonconformist leaders. One of these was, of course, the leader of the Passive Resistance group, another was Scott Lidgett, who had just become President of the National Council of Evangelical Free Churches. A Bill was drafted, its main features being the transfer of voluntary schools to local education authorities. Scott Lidgett was in complete agreement with the proposals, but he recognized on the one hand the dangers of a too-autocratic control by the State of so essentially a human undertaking as education, and on the other the complete opposition that would be forthcoming from Roman Catholics. That the opposition was not likely to be so dangerous from Anglican quarters was due to the closer relationsip with Anglican clergy which Scott Lidgett had been forming by his personal efforts. As President of the Free Church Council he had to travel all over the country, and he found himself conducting services at one hour, holding diplomatic conferences with clergy of all denominations at another, and trying to persuade people in general of the merits of the proposed Education Bill at another. These public performances alone provided a whole-time job, but unknown to the public were other discussions, even more delicate—meetings with Mr Augustine Birrell, the President of the comparatively new and therefore critically regarded Board of Education, with Mr Lloyd George, with Dr Clifford, and with the Prime Minister himself. When the Bill was introduced to the House, these private discussions in London became even more crucial. Again, as in the 1902 controversy, he soon realized that a certain amount of compromise, both political and denominational, was going to be essential, and here he found himself again in a difficult position, especially with Mr J. Hirst Hallowell, a former Congregational minister, who was determined to allow no concessions at all. Scott Lidgett worked, talked, and (such was the man) prayed. But it was all to no avail. The Roman Catholics were too deeply entrenched, the House of Lords was still thinking in terms of the previous century, and political bargaining ultimately defeated its own object. At the end of 1906 the Bill was withdrawn.

In 1908 Dr McKenna, who had succeeded Mr Birrell at the Board of Education, made another attempt, the main feature of his Bill being the giving of rate aid only to schools which provided undenominational teaching. Voluntary schools were to be invited to transfer themselves to local education authorities. If they did not accept the invitation, rate aid would be withdrawn. 'Contracting out', this was called. Scott Lidgett immediately pointed out the difficulties, emphasizing the points mentioned earlier: that education was no longer an affair of mere instruction, that it included social and medical aid, and scholarship schemes. Schools which contracted out in this way would be denying themselves of these essential ancillary services, and no denomination could afford to provide them from its own resources. Naturally, his view was shared by Anglicans, Roman Catholics, and Nonconformists alike, and for once the Churches showed a united front against the Government. The Bill was withdrawn. A further attempt by another President of the Board of Education, Mr Runciman, was no more successful.

In an essay of this length, space does not permit one to deal with all the educational movements and achievements on which Scott Lidgett had some influence. The educational trends at the beginning of the century have been dealt with at some length, however, because at that time Scott Lidgett was in his prime, he was setting the pace, as it were, for Nonconformity and establishing a standard. He was not the only Methodist involved in that, of course, but he would not have reached the eminent position he came to hold in education had his work not been outstanding. The place of religion in education has never been more vitally important than it is today, and the fact that Methodism has co-operated so strongly and so realistically with the State's efforts to provide better and wider educational facilities at all levels is due in no small measure to Scott Lidgett's work, for it was in those early years of the century rather than in the 1930s and 1940s that the real possibilities of State education were being explored, though realization did not come till 1944. We shall return to that later.

There was another matter on which Scott Lidgett had strong views: the supreme importance of the teacher. His election to the Vice-Chancellorship of the University of London gave him the opportunity to press for a closer relationship between the University and teacher-training colleges. It was needed. As Professor Lester Smith has written: 'It was a tragedy for education that the universities, like the public schools, for long cold-shouldered the elementary school teacher, largely because they were allergic to any educational enterprise associated with the State.'[13] Such championship of the training-colleges by Scott Lidgett was a natural outcome of his view of education, for there is no gainsaying the fact that even today there is a great gulf fixed between the teacher in the primary school and the teacher in the secondary grammar school, to say nothing of the public school. Even more was this the case earlier in the century.

In October 1918, just as the first World War was nearing its end, Scott Lidgett wrote an article for the *Contemporary Review* which was welcomed as the official pronouncement of the LCC Progressive Party, to whose leadership he had recently been elected. That article was entitled 'London after the War'. It was a practical man's vision of what could be, and of what must be if London was to continue as the recognized first city of the world. Amongst the matters needing urgently to be tackled was education. 'The main equipment of life is education', he wrote. 'Every child must enjoy its full birthright of education and opportunity', but this could only be done if there was an adequate supply of teachers, if the size of the classes was reduced, if school buildings and equipment were

[13] *Education in Great Britain*, p. 149.

improved, if the educational course for children was sufficiently long (a leaving age of fourteen was not sufficient), if there was ample provision and careful co-ordination of all grades of education with every possible facility for a gifted child to climb from one grade to another, if there was a more enlightened curriculum for the various grades, so that the not-so-gifted too could realize themselves, and if there was a more realistic approach in the schools to the trades and careers likely to follow school days. Concisely and clearly, he outlined the needs, but he did stress one need more than all others—the need for highly qualified teachers who had entered their profession as a vocation. Only by giving teachers a higher status in the social hierarchy, by offering better salaries and better training facilities would such teachers be found.

A reading of that article today reveals the writer's grasp of reality, but it was not till the publication of the Hadow Report in 1926 that many of the views expressed found official voice and a wider public. As Scott Lidgett himself has said, though in no boastful fashion: 'I took the lead by publishing a progressive policy of reconstruction....' It is scarcely surprising that we find him in close touch with the various movements for educational reform even as late as 1944, and in no one of those movements was he more influential than in that which led to better methods of training teachers. Inspired and guided as he was by the memories and the example of John Scott, he was especially satisfied when in 1926 a change in the organization of teacher-training was officially mooted. By that time he was a Senator of the University of London (having been elected in 1922), and from that time he was a champion in that assembly of the needs of young men and women anxious to become teachers. In 1926 the Board of Education proposed to hand over the responsibility of examining training-college students to joint committees in which both the Universities and the training-colleges were to be represented. This was to be done on a regional basis. The Universities were not particularly interested and the whole scheme was somewhat vague, but up and down the country were men and women who saw great possibilities. One of these was the LCC Chief Education

Officer (Sir George Gater). He approached Scott Lidgett, who readily consented to act as intermediary between the LCC and London University. A draft scheme was approved in the following year, and in 1928 the Training College Delegacy was established with Scott Lidgett as a member nominated by the University Senate. This body awarded Teachers' Certificates on the results of an examination conducted jointly by training-college lecturers and University examiners. A link between University and training-colleges had thus been forged, but it must be admitted that on the whole it did not produce the closer working relationship that had been hoped for, nor did it bridge the gulf of which Scott Lidgett had for long been conscious between elementary and secondary schools, since the work of the Delegacy was specifically concerned with the examination of teachers for elementary schools. The McNair Report thus states the problem: 'The (training) colleges were arranged in groups and brought into an examination relationship with the universities by the establishment of joint examination Boards, each consisting of representatives of the university and of the colleges concerned. The fact that the several colleges of a group are all represented on the same Joint Board has not, in general, resulted in their having any closer relations with one another, save in the matter of examinations, than they had when they were more directly under the Board of Education. There is no co-operation between them about staffing, nor do they share amenities.'

This was regrettable, and no one was better aware of the impasse than Scott Lidgett, who in 1930 became Vice-Chancellor of the University of London. Addressing the students of Westminster and Southlands Colleges in 1909, he had said: 'The guarantee of all such higher influence in the schools lies not so much in formal lessons as in the character of the teacher. In every sphere of life, personality is the most effective influence, but in the school it is all-important. Children are affected, one way or another, much more powerfully by contact with their teachers than in any other way. If noble suggestions and elevating ideals are to possess and mould the life of a child, it will be for the most part because they so live in the teacher as to be conveyed, both consciously and unconsciously, to the children. Each one of you is called to be a representative personality, concentrating in your character and influence the highest ideals of those who send you forth—Christ, the Church, the nation. Much depends on what you know; more on what you are; most of all on what you are becoming. In all men character is the supreme concern.' But in saying that, he must have been conscious that, however sound the life and teaching provided in the training-colleges, just because they were training-colleges they lacked the larger vision, the more profound thought, the more alive stimuli which a university provided. It had long been a matter of deep regret that the Universities concerned themselves so little, in many cases not at all, with the teaching profession as such. This deep-seated conviction was to have a dramatic climax some years later.

In 1942 a Royal Commission under the chairmanship of Sir Arnold McNair was appointed to inquire into the supply, recruiting and training of teachers and youth leaders, for the new President of the Board of Education (Mr R. A. Butler) also realized that without properly trained teachers the most perfect Education Act was merely futile. The Commission reported in 1944 and advocated the setting up of area training organizations. But just as there had been considerable differences of opinion and practice in the organization of the joint examining boards, so on the Commission itself there was a strong difference of opinion as to the exact form these area training organizations should take. One half advocated the establishment of University Institutes of Education (Scheme A) which would involve a major change in the whole organization and administration of teacher training; the other half advocated a modification of the joint examining board system (Scheme B).

Scott Lidgett was keenly interested. He saw in Scheme B an all too familiar compromise solution which would inevitably leave the training-colleges as much out of touch with the Universities as before. He saw in Scheme A an opportunity to awaken the Universities to a new conception of their function as teaching-bodies. He was an old man by this time, but he was still a Senator of the University of London; he was still one of the most influential members of the Metropolitan Training Colleges Delegacy; he was still ready for a fight if need be. It soon became obvious that in London at any rate there was great and influential hostility to Scheme A. Usually, matters of great moment are settled in Committee, and only go before the larger body for ratification, but that was not so in this case. Until the very meeting of the Senate in which this matter had to be decided no one knew which way the vote would go. Scott Lidgett hobbled to his seat with his now-familiar sticks. He listened to the debate as it waxed hot, for already strong feelings had been aroused. At last, he got to his feet. Quietly at first, practised debater that he was, he put the case for the establishment of a London Institute of Education, surpassing himself in persuasive argument and long-sighted vision, but before long he had forgotten the niceties of debate, and the preacher—perhaps the prophet—came to the fore. With increasing fervour, he reminded his hearers of the function of a University, of the fact that no University could exist without a body of dedicated and highly qualified teachers to produce the human personalities which were the life-blood of any University. Carried away by his own convictions, he brandished his two sticks in the air as he shouted to the Senators that the University of London had a duty to establish its own Institute of Education. The vote was taken and the Institute of Education came into being. It was largely that impassioned speech of utter sincerity that carried the day.

Things were far from easy in its infancy, but Scott Lidgett was not content to sway his hearers in a large assembly. He worked quietly behind the scenes, and it was largely due to his methodical, firm influence that under Dr G. B. Jeffery the Institute of Education came gradually to hold the honoured place in the University of London that it has today.

It would be interesting to know which public appointment gave Scott Lidgett the greatest satisfaction. He was not an ambitious man in the usual sense of the word, but, as we have seen, he took very real pleasure in his election to the London

School Board, though the pleasure was not entirely for himself but for the recognition which he felt it marked of the work his Settlement was doing. His election to the Vice-Chancellorship of the largest University in the world brought him, one supposes, to the top rung of his particular educational ladder, and there is no denying the fact that he enjoyed the eminence. He liked a sense of power—he was very human in that liking—but he never misused the power. Perhaps it would be more accurate to say that he enjoyed the use of powers. It would certainly explain that zest for life which was so peculiarly his. Be that as it may, Scott Lidgett found himself much in the limelight, and in many different roles. It is important to remember, however, that much of his most important work for education, and particularly for religious education, lay in quiet work 'behind the scenes'—sometimes in his own room off the Jamaica Road in Bermondsey, sometimes at County Hall, sometimes in Whitehall, sometimes at Lambeth Palace, sometimes at the Athenaeum (for which he was proposed by Archbishop Davidson), or in one of the all too numerous ramifications of the University of London before the chief offices were brought together in the fine building which houses them today.

One of the matters that concerned him most was 'the dual system' in education, linked as it was with his wider concern about sectarian differences between the Churches. In the early years of this century the problem seemed insuperable; by 1935 Scott Lidgett was able to write: 'The need of making adequate provision for religious education, without any violation of the conscience or sacrifice of the interests either of teachers or scholars, is growingly felt by Christians of every denomination, and, I think, by men of goodwill beyond the borders.' That this was so was due in no small measure to his untiring, but so often frustrated, talks 'behind the scenes'. Relations between the Anglicans and the Evangelical Free Churches in particular were becoming closer. This is well illustrated today in the widespread use of 'Agreed Syllabuses'. Unfortunately, Scott Lidgett himself makes but a passing reference to these in his own writings, but the fact that the idea, once started by Cambridgeshire in 1924, became so popular, is certainly evidence of that closer working, and the name of Scott Lidgett must be associated with it. By the outbreak of war in 1939 matters had indeed so far advanced that the demand for purely secular education had receded. War itself finally set the stage for the production of a new Education Act.

It is difficult, even after a lapse of years, to obtain a clear picture of the thoughts and emotions which led to the passing of the 1944 Education Act. Emotionally, it might be said to have been inspired by the horror and consternation that swept the placid backwaters of the country when the mass evacuation of the larger cities was ordered in 1939. A well-conceived theoretical plan was pushed piecemeal into operation and resulted in chaos. This is not the place to deal with that particular wartime misfortune. Dr Scott Lidgett chose deliberately —and characteristically—to stay in his own room at Bermondsey. But the results of that mass evacuation were far-reaching. Respectable people in small country towns then saw for the first time the products of the much-vaunted educational system: the manners and discipline of children were not in fact unduly bad—in their own schools, their own surroundings, and with their own teachers—but these children were suddenly cut off from those moderately reliable restraints and from their parents. The net result was shocked horror and a rude awakening for many people in England. That was the ground in which the seeds of a new growth of national education might well be sown with some chance of their striking roots and flourishing. The President of the Board of Education (then Mr Ramsbottom) and his Parliamentary Secretary had realized in any case that new measures would be needed for the education of the country's children after the war. Here was the popular incentive.

The first real move came, however, from the Churches. The Anglican Archbishops, the Roman Catholic Archbishop of Westminster and the Moderator of the Free Church Federal Council united in drawing up a memorial in 1940 entitled 'A Christian Basis for Peace'. Scott Lidgett, who was even then the grand old man of the Free Church Federal Council, had naturally been consulted and was taking the keenest possible interest in the stirrings of new ideas. Later, the Archbishop of York (William Temple) put forward further proposals as Chairman of an Anglican Conference meeting that year in Malvern. These public utterances only concealed the great amount of discussion and planning—and dreaming—that was going on. From the Nonconformist point of view one of the disturbing factors was Scott Lidgett! In one sense he had outgrown Methodism, possibly Nonconformity as a whole. It was the Rev. Dr A. W. Harrison who in those pre-1944 discussions most truly represented Nonconformity. This is no criticism of the man who had for so long been regarded as the chief pillar of his Church, especially in regard to the social aspects of Methodism; rather is it a comment on the long years of struggle that had preceded the 1944 Act, years in which Scott Lidgett, more than any other Nonconformist, had become more statesman than pastor.

Elsewhere in this book a full account is given of Scott Lidgett's tireless attempt to bring the denominations of the Christian Church into closer harmony. Nowhere did he regret sectarian differences more than in the sphere of education, and for that very reason he grew increasingly suspect to his fellow Nonconformists. Especially, perhaps, did he enjoy the friendship of leaders in the Anglican Church, and his frequent meetings with them—at Lambeth Palace and in the Athenaeum —were not regarded with favour by Nonconformists who feared lest still more educational 'rights' might be sacrificed. Looking back on events now, one can see that so far as the 1944 Act is concerned, State policy concerning the place of religion in education is in line with all that Scott Lidgett worked for, and that Methodism, more than the rest of Nonconformity, wholly supported those views. One wonders whether that would have been so had not Scott Lidgett refused adamantly to join Dr Clifford's Passive Resistance at the beginning of the century, had he not by casual words here and carefully prepared addresses there built up in the minds of Methodists a broader view of education.

Nevertheless, despite that influence which was certainly very real, there was a great deal of suspicion lest Scott Lidgett should 'give away too much'. William Temple, when Archbishop of Canterbury, once at least seemed to feel that the hostility of the Nonconformists was less than in fact it was, and it was Dr A. W. Harrison, then Secretary of the Methodist Education Committee, who at a meeting in Leeds forcibly reminded him and other Anglicans that fires were still smouldering in Nonconformity. The subject of the meeting was religious education, and the talk around the committee table was polite and amiable in the extreme. Closely in touch as he was with the whole of Methodism—and with the N.U.T.—Dr Harrison found himself carried away by that 'divine passion' which we occasionally glimpsed. It was all very well, he said, to have matters politely discussed and arranged in the tranquillity of a committee room, but outside, up and down the country in Nonconformity, were real grievances, bottled up no doubt, but nevertheless potentially volcanic. Perhaps he also had sensed a too conciliatory hand of friendship being extended to the Church of England by Scott Lidgett. It was probably that outspoken comment by Dr Harrison which brought home to the Anglicans the fact that Nonconformist grievances still existed. There is no need to pursue the matter. Suffice it that the very greatness of the work that Scott Lidgett did in the 1920s and 1930s in extending friendship caused him to be seriously suspected by his nonconformist friends. Nor should one imagine, as a reading of these pages may suggest, that Scott Lidgett was the only Methodist educationist. We are fortunate in having a number whose counsels have been sought and views respected, but amongst them Scott Lidgett towers.

It is not too much to say, however, that had it not been for that closer relationship, the passing of the Education Act of 1944 might well have been as hotly and bitterly contested as was that of 1902. On 15th August 1941 a deputation of thirty-three persons, perhaps deliberately adopting shock tactics, waited on Mr R. A. Butler, the newly appointed President of the Board of Education. It must have made matters difficult for Mr Butler, new as he was to his post, but nevertheless it was an opportune time for the Churches to make clear to the nation the views that had been thrashed out in private conversations and arguments. These views have become known as the Archbishops' Five Points. They were outlined by the leader of the deputation, the Archbishop of Canterbury (Dr Lang). They were:

(*a*) The need for Christian education for all, subject to the conscience clause;
(*b*) The need for more definite encouragement of religious studies in the Teachers' Certificate;
(*c*) Abolition of the clause which required Scripture to be taught in primary schools only at the beginning or end of a session;
(*d*) Inspection of religious teaching by His Majesty's Inspectors;
(*e*) The opening of each school day with worship.

Dr Scott Lidgett, leading the Nonconformists, and the deputation's second speaker, claims that the Churches were unanimous in putting forward these five points. 'Unanimous' was hardly the right word, but, as Lord Sankey, another member of the deputation, claimed, there was indeed a more united front being shown by that deputation than had ever appeared since the State started to interest itself in education over a hundred years before. As far as Anglicanism and Methodism were concerned, the chief credit for that rested with Scott Lidgett. It was a former Archbishop of Canterbury (Dr Randall Davidson) who had once said to Scott Lidgett: 'You see, you understand us.' It was shortly after this deputation had been heard that the Government was in fact warned not to listen to Scott Lidgett as the voice of Nonconformity. Nevertheless, he had to be listened to as an educationist, and it was he who during the hearing of the five points insisted that neither His Majesty's Inspectors nor anyone else could inspect religious teaching without considering at the same time both method and content. Some members of the deputation appeared to think they could!

During the hearing of that deputation, the thoughts of many must have veered to the unhappy quarrels which had threatened the passing of the 1902 Act and caused the complete foundering of the proposed 'Birrell Act' of 1906. The President of the Board of Education voiced such thoughts as he reminded the deputation of the difficulty of religious tests. Scott Lidgett spoke metaphorically of 'sunken rocks', and subsequently made it clear that he did at least represent Nonconformity in regarding the chief of those rocks as the unfair amount of financial aid which Roman Catholicism and Anglicanism were obtaining from the State by comparison with Nonconformity. It was the Parliamentary Secretary to the Board of Education (Mr J. Chuter Ede) who, using the same metaphor, said that the tide was then flowing strongly enough to carry an Education Bill over any sunken rocks that might exist. He was right. But the fact that the tide, so far as the Churches were concerned, was flowing strongly was, in no small measure, due to two men: William Temple and Scott Lidgett.

Whatever that deputation did or did not do, it made clear to the Government that no Education Act would pass which did not take cognizance of the genuine demand then existing for Christianity (embracing all denominations) to be a main element in its structure. Perhaps it was the realization of this which led the President of the Board of Education to surprise laymen and Churchmen alike by asking the Archbishop of Canterbury to close the meeting with prayer; perhaps he had taken Scott Lidgett's claim concerning unanimity at its face value. The fact remains that never before had a Parliamentary leader asked a deputation to pray together. Prayer was indeed needed. Mr Butler wrote to Dr Temple in 1942: 'If all the main partners do not solve this question together on this occasion—however patient we may have to be—I rather wonder who will find a way out ever.' *The Times*, no less realistic in its interpretation of popular thought, wrote: 'The time for a settlement is now or never.'

Scott Lidgett never grew old. Of course, he came to looking old; he hobbled into committees on two sticks, and he carried his grandfather's old plaid rug around with him. But there was a sharp surprise awaiting the man who rashly assumed any real ageing of the mental faculties. He might be said to belong to that small group of men whom Baudelaire labelled 'genius'—

men who at will were able to recollect their own youth. To the end of his days he was aware of progress and was always alert for new methods of achieving more. With all his administrative ability and acumen, he kept close to the members of humanity whom he served (though members of committees on which he sat might be pardoned for not sharing that view!). Especially where little children were concerned, he showed a compassion which in some men might have appeared as mere sentimentality, but which in Scott Lidgett was lifted above that. He was fond of recalling the bad old days rather than the good old days. 'When I was young', he would say, 'the children had not enough to eat, they had no shoes on their feet.' All that has changed, and he was modestly proud of the part he had played in the change. Few could fail to be touched by the nodding, smiling old man as he looked on the children gathered round his waiting car after he had received the Freedom of the Borough of Bermondsey, or as he came slowly down the aisle after taking a service at Westminster College between the standing students and murmured to right and left: 'God bless you.' Unlike so many men, old in years, whose minds are constantly turning backward to a glorious past, he had the capacity of absorbing the best from the past, of registering the novelties of the present, of assessing them, regrouping them in his mind and of using those that opened up new avenues of development for attaining ideals which he never forsook. In his Address at the Memorial Service, the Rev. Walter J. Noble said: 'He never believed . . . that the sturdy breed of strong and good men had died out with his generation. He believed in youth, entered into its generous instincts and impulses, encouraged it in every way, and was abreast of all those movements which seek to improve man's lot.' His interest in films and all the paraphernalia of visual education of which mention has been made above is evidence of this trait of character.

It was typical of him that he gave great practical help in the very last years of his life to the Quarry Centre of psychotherapy, founded in 1948 by Miss Ruth Simpson as a child welfare centre at Epsom, but broadening out as the work developed to include direct enlightenment and instruction for parents and teachers who faced practical problems of childhood and adolescence, and so strengthening family life.

It was perhaps chance that brought Scott Lidgett into contact with this work, though he himself would undoubtedly have described it as yet another instance of divine guidance. The point needs no stressing. What is important is that his interest in educational and remedial psychology was the logical development of his own faith and practice. In his very early years he had come to realize the importance of a new religious approach to mental development. At first he had not been sure of his approach. 'I was determined', he said in his early years at Bermondsey, 'that these people should learn Greek!' But gradually, through disappointment and argument, through the way of first-hand experience, he came to know the right approach. He showed it in his work at Bermondsey, on the London School Board, as a member of the London County Council, as a Senator of the University of London, as Vice-Chancellor of that University, and in the lead he gave to the establishment of Institutes of Education. His work was, in fact, Christian Socialism on the mental plane.

When he retired from Bermondsey, Scott Lidgett went to live near Epsom and there in 1950 he became Chairman of the Quarry Centre. He regarded that work, not as a hobby undertaken in old age, but as a further expression of his creed. Having convinced himself that this was no mere 'fad', but that remarkable cures in maladjusted children were indeed being wrought, he gave his own mind to the work. He paid public tribute to the vision of a number of qualified people led by Miss Ruth Simpson, but he realized that organization was needed for carrying on the work. A Constitution was therefore drawn up and a Committee and Treasurer appointed. Characteristically, in other words, he was not carried away by idealism; he appreciated the practical difficulties and himself took steps to help. He interested the local education authorities, training-colleges, and schools, for he realized through his own keen perception and through his experience of social problems what too many teachers and parents still fail to realize: that much of the work of education is not straightforward teaching and development, but is remedial in nature, that mental and spiritual growth may not be possible until some expert psychological help has been given in readjusting the whole personality. Financial backing was essential for work of this sort, and, through his friend Lord Macmillan, Scott Lidgett persuaded the Pilgrim Trust to make a substantial grant. There can have been few men of ninety-seven who have wrestled till the early hours of a day with such a problem and who, having come to certain conclusions, have then dictated immediately after breakfast a statement about the work which led the Pilgrim Trust to reply in effect: 'We do not do this as a general rule, but . . .'

That work at the Quarry Centre, small as it may appear when viewed against the broad canvas of his earlier activities, and the happy sense which it gave him of continuing to perform constructive work long after most men have retired from great activities, brought real joy to him and to those with whom he worked in the closing months of his life. It was appropriate that in 1954 a 'Scott Lidgett Memorial Room' was dedicated to his work at the Quarry Centre, for it set a religious seal to work which, though officially mental in scope, was yet predominantly spiritual.

He recognized the need for a training in leadership, and that was one reason why the wide gap between the Universities and teacher-training so distressed him; he was a hard task-master, most of all to himself, and made himself conversant with every detail of any organization he served, for he appreciated how easily one detail out of place might wreck the whole; yet, practical visionary that he was, he never lost sight of the main issue. Whatever may have been the criticism levelled against him for so resolutely striving for increasingly close relations with other denominations, he will nevertheless be remembered as an outstanding champion of the Free Churches in the educational field, simply because he had that ability to assess the situation of the moment. He was perhaps the greatest diplomat that Methodism has ever produced, knowing intuitively when he could afford to give and when he must stand firm at all costs. He early found the ground wherein his soul's anchor could remain with no fear of dragging, and every threatened encroachment on the place of religion in education he fought with every power he possessed.

In a man so able, so hardworking, so sincere and so influential as Scott Lidgett, there could be no divergence between his view of education and his contribution to it. He worked steadily for the more realistic vision of the human family and its recognition of the Fatherhood of God, and, naturally enough, he found it nowhere better expressed than in the Settlements such as Toynbee Hall, Oxford House, the Women's University Settlement, Mansfield House, and his own Bermondsey. It is fitting to close this chapter with words written by Scott Lidgett himself in 1938: 'The present tendency... is to react against the conception upon which the Settlements have been based. The class self-sufficiency of the industrial majority is a tenet that, perhaps naturally, is widely held. To destroy the present system, in order to effect a more satisfactory reconstruction, is the avowed aim of a minority by whom "class consciousness" is fostered. The policy that is thus originated and stimulated contradicts the fundamental principles of social wholeness, of ordered process, and of mutual self-giving, upon which the Settlements have rested, and which they have sought to embody in their work. The result of this contradiction is to engender practical materialism, with its trust in mechanism, its externality, and its reliance upon the force of mass movements directed to political action. It remains true, however, that true progress must be spiritual in order to be truly social, and that it must be God-centred in order to call forth the best in men in fellowship with one another because they are in fellowship with God, and in partnership with His ordered purpose for mankind. Hence, if disaster and disappointment are to be avoided, social ideals must still be dependent upon, and inspired by, the Idea of God, as this has been given in our Lord and Saviour Jesus Christ.'

F. C. PRITCHARD

THE PUBLIC SERVANT

CHAPTER FIVE

THE PUBLIC SERVANT

ONE is tempted sometimes to wonder what someone might have been had he not been what he was. In the case of Scott Lidgett there is no place for doubt. His gifts, his idiosyncrasy, his mental outlook, must have compelled him toward public life as the magnet draws the iron. His earliest ambition was the Law. What a barrister he would have made! Imagination hears him and sees him in wig and gown thundering at the jury, and with unruffled dignity replying to the interruptions of the Bench. But it was to be among the prophets, not in the Law, that his destiny was cast. Yet those same qualities which would probably have crowned a legal career with a judge's robes, were used in the wider service of God to which he was as truly called as he was to the Christian Ministry. Some, like one of our most famous Q.C.s of today, have left the Church to fulfil their legal or administrative careers. Scott Lidgett, with that devouring industry which carried him through a life that embraced twice the content of an average man's labours, continued his churchmanship and with it the higher services of citizenship.

How he did it without a breakdown in health right to the end was a mystery to his friends. I recollect complaining in a Methodist District Synod that the probationers were expected to supply book lists of much more reading than any average young man in a circuit could be expected to accomplish. Lidgett flattened out my objection from the chair with the words: 'Are there not twelve hours in the day?' For him it was more like sixteen! I warned him once that no man could hope to continue the strain of work he undertook and keep his health. 'Why not?' was his retort. 'I eat well, sleep well, and do not worry.' At any rate he proved right. His last days were spent in a nursing-home at Epsom where I live, and I was able to see him from time to time. Only a week or two before his death I found him sitting in his dressing-gown by his bedside dictating letters to his secretary! Someone invented a story about him which was exactly what would have happened were such a thing possible. It was that the Angel of Death, seeing in his records Lidgett's ninety-eight years, reproached himself for overlooking the fact, and silently presented himself in the doctor's study, saying in sepulchral tones, 'Come with me'! Without raising his head from his work, the doctor replied: 'Go away. Don't worry me, I'm busy!' And the grim messenger fled.

It has been said that many people think themselves into old age and retirement, and probably that is true. No such thoughts ever troubled Lidgett. He calmly ignored the passing years and went on. During his later days he became much crippled and moved slowly upon sticks. The doctor was evidently of the opinion that, as the Psalmist says, the Lord 'taketh no pleasure in the legs of a man', for when I remarked to him that I was sorry to see him so handicapped, he replied: 'All my life my legs have taken me where I willed that they should, and they will still do so!'

His indomitable spirit carried him on when his body weakened. Once he got up to leave a committee at the Central Hall Westminster before it closed, and I could not help feeling nervous about his walking unaided down the steep steps to the street, but knew better than to offer assistance! An idea struck me and I hastened after him, and taking his arm casually, said: 'I was looking for the opportunity to tell you that some eight or ten years ago, the *British Weekly* asked me to write a short account of your career, for filing. They wrote again lately to say that this was now out of date in some respects, and would I revise it?' 'Well,' said Lidgett, 'and have you done so?' I replied that I had. 'Then', said he, 'I hope you'll have to do it again later on!' He never thought of himself as at the end of life or work. Day by day he went on. Illness troubled him but little. Breakdowns were unknown to him. I never heard him plead fatigue or over-work.

In the last visits I made, he always seemed to be busy, and what struck me particularly was that his interests were never in the past, as the interests of so many old people are, but in the present, and what he wanted to know was what was being done at the various committees which he was now unable to attend. When I was able to tell him, he would ponder a moment and then give me an admirable opinion of the wisdom, or otherwise, of the actions that had been taken. He was still there in spirit when he could no longer be there in body. On the last occasion when I saw him, a few days before he died, he gave me advice I shall try to remember: 'Speak slower and speak louder, Waterhouse; you ought to have some years yet in which to say what you want to say!' I did not think then I should hear the familiar voice of my old chief no more, but it spoke then, as always, words of wisdom.

For public life in bodies like the London County Council and University, the equipment of character and temperament Lidgett possessed was ideal. First and foremost he had a sense of vocation. He was not deeply concerned with any personal ambition. He held that he must serve the Kingdom of God above all other duties and he firmly believed that social service was divine service. As I heard him say, on one occasion: 'That the work of the Church is primarily spiritual, I do not for one moment dispute. But I am not willing that it should be merely an ambulance to gather up the casualties of our industrial system, without being equally anxious to lessen the causes of those casualties.' To do so was his motive in all the forms of public service which he fulfilled.

He had a commanding presence and clear voice. He was a reasoner rather than an orator, and yet at times he would give voice to a sentence which touched the imagination and held the memory. On one occasion I recall that he was speaking of the type of man who was produced by the conditions of life in Bermondsey's drab materialism, which buried the divine spark that is the mark of the Creator in all His creation. But he added: 'I have seen times when the ploughshare of sorrow and adversity has broken up the hard and trampled ground and the spark beneath, released, has leapt upward to the Eternal Fire of Love.'

Lidgett had the remarkable power of following the longest

and dreariest discussions with apparent interest. I have sat with him in meetings at the University when business concerning some Faculty which, frankly, was Greek to me, or rather worse, was being discussed. I have been lost, not to say bored, and quite unable to unravel the discussion or understand what it was all about. But Lidgett, gravely listening, would suddenly come out with some point which showed that he, at least, had mastered the obscurities which had all but sent me to sleep. I imagine that at least a quarter of Lidgett's working life was spent in committee rooms of all kinds, but he never seemed lost or uninterested in this chastening form of democratic government.

He was not noted for pulpit brevity, though in later life he learned it, in so much that, right up to the end, he was wont to preach to the girls at Farringtons School and to be popular too. In committee, however, he did not speak too often or too long, and I never recollect him making a pointless interruption. In this respect the old saying was true concerning him, that what he touched he adorned. Neither assertive nor apologetic, neither dominant nor insignificant, he made his contribution to whatever task he was called, both as master and as servant of assemblies.

THE LONDON COUNTY COUNCIL

The chief spring of interest in all Lidgett's public work was Christian education. His educational work is dealt with elsewhere in this volume, and it will be enough to say that he had prepared himself for the work of the LCC by membership for many years of civic welfare and educational bodies, so that when he entered the Council as an alderman in 1905, he was no stranger to the committee room and the debating chamber.

Next year came the overwhelming Liberal triumph, which seemed to many a veritable beginning of the Kingdom of heaven on earth. It was strange that this victory for the progressive forces in the country was indirectly one of the reasons for the fall of the Progressive Party in the LCC. The sweeping parliamentary victory of the Liberals carried into the House of Commons the cream of the Progressives on the LCC. Some resigned their seats on that body, others remained, but, not surprisingly, with slackened interest in it, as distinctly second to parliamentary duties.

In 1907 disaster befell the Progressives. The opposition party, who chose, one thinks with unwitting humour, to call themselves Moderates, had been chagrined by the Liberal parliamentary triumph of the previous year, and staged an elaborate campaign for the seizure of London. They chose the old cry of extravagance. The Progressives had planned an LCC estate at Norbury and had in part built it, with bricks allegedly defective. The Moderates sent lorries with 'Norbury bricks' parading London in derision. But the chief plank in the somewhat discreditable platform was the new County Hall which the Progressives had started to build on the splendid site upon the Embankment, near the south side of Westminster Bridge. Now that the Festival Hall has become its neighbour, the whole side of the river at that point has become worthy of the great city. Then it was a mixture of slum and factory.

The Moderates rushed into battle with the slogan 'The Wastrels' Palace', assuring the voters that these wicked squandermaniacs were building a magnificent and costly place for themselves at the ratepayers' expense. 'It's your money they are taking', they shouted. The 'rag Press', with its halfpenny papers, was growing in power and set itself to create a vast stunt on behalf of the Moderates, who now were appearing under the title of 'Municipal Reformers'. The campaign succeeded, the Progressives were driven out, and Municipal Reformers held the Council in their hands for twenty-seven years before they fell before the growing strength of Labour.

Of course the Norbury estate and the County Hall were not continued by London's new masters. But when after the first World War, it was essential that London should have more housing and a civic centre, new estates, less conveniently situated than Norbury, had to be developed, and the County Hall had to be finished. By this time the vast increase of prices which followed the War made the completion of the hall cost several times the amount it would have cost had the Progressives been able to complete it, as they would have done, before 1914.

The ratepayers ended therefore by paying considerably more for their civic centre as the result of listening to the discreditable campaign of 1907. Another plank in the programme of the Anti-Progressives was opposition to municipal control of electricity, which once more indicates that the Municipal Reform Party was 'the home of lost causes'. But before London discovered that, many years passed and much money was wasted.

Mr McKinnon Wood, the defeated leader of 1907, gave way to Sir John Benn, till a coalition for war emergencies was established in 1917. On Benn's retirement in 1918, Lidgett was elected leader of the Progressive Party. With Reginald McKenna and Augustine Birrell, he rendered great service to education, which was still the battle-ground of various parties, particularly on the question of religious teaching. Their efforts to find a settlement on this point were described by some wag as offering the choice of religion, irreligion, and Birreligion!

Lidgett's duties at the LCC occasionally clashed with those elsewhere; the marvel was that they clashed so little. On one occasion, however, Lidgett was at the County Council on the morning of the Ministerial session of the old Third London District of the Wesleyan Methodist Church, over which he presided for so many years. The Rev. Joseph Dixon deputized for him. It was then part of the synod's duty to see that every minister answered the question—'Do you believe and preach our doctrines?' The names were read and the usual affirmative replies were given, till the secretary read the name of the Rev. William Spiers, a good and able man who was theologically a strong fundamentalist. Mr Spiers woke the drowsy synod to startled attention by loudly answering 'No'. The chairman naturally imagined he had mistaken the question, but was promptly assured he had not. The perplexed Mr Dixon asked for an explanation and was told: 'Sir, I hear my brethren saying "Yes" to this question, and I believe they are truthful and honourable men. Yet they believe and preach what I do not and never shall do. Hence I can only answer "No". Mr Dixon decided to leave the matter till Lidgett returned. The question was then repeated and the same reply came from

Mr Spiers. The doctor's wrath was aroused, and, rising from his chair, he thundered: 'This is frivolous.' Mr Spiers pressed his point, but the doctor would have none of it. 'It is frivolous. Put him down as saying "Yes".' Mr Spiers gave up the struggle, and the secretary made his negative an affirmative. Lidgett was never at a loss in the chairs he occupied, whether the presidential chair of the Conference, or the Vice-Chancellor's chair of the University, or the chair of an LCC committee, or a Church synod.

Although the Progressives were a dwindling minority on the Council when Lidgett took over the leadership, he showed his statesmanship by his policy which he advocated in the manifesto published in the *Contemporary Review* in October 1918, envisaging London after the War, which at that time had not ended. He pointed out that London was outgrowing the county of London. The latter had a population of 4½ million, the population of greater London was 7¼ million. He envisaged a greater LCC to embrace greater London and unify its very diverse administration by various separate bodies. Lidgett was before his time. The various county councils were in no mood to see their powers taken over, and they combined to push Lidgett's proposals into the background. Yet today most of the points he advocated have in one way or another come to pass, though not always as he would have had them. Unified transport was one of his demands, but he deplored the 'autocratic powers' of London Passenger Transport.

Lidgett's leadership on the Council was that of the commander of a retreating army, knowing itself defeated and losing in numbers and in heart. It says much for his courage and generalship that he carried on undaunted for ten years, until the rump of the once great Progressive Party wound itself up and handed over the task of the cause of Liberalism in London to the London Liberal Federation, much against the will of its courageous leader.

Lidgett was, however, spared from the unwelcome task of surrender. He had a safe seat, presumably, at Rotherhithe, where the work of the Bermondsey Settlement had given him, very justly, a good reputation. But at the 1922 election he was opposed by Labour, and, amongst other things, his opponents took advantage of a local strike, which the men regarded as a lock-out, that had put some hundreds of dockers out of work. The employers' foreman was a Wesleyan, and the charge was spread along the waterside that Lidgett was 'blacklegging' on behalf of the employers. The bitterness always engendered at the time of a strike proved fatal. Lidgett was defeated. He was immediately offered the position of alderman, which he accepted to the satisfaction even of his opponents on the Council. His remaining years were more tranquil, and no highly controversial matters disturbed the usual routine of duties. In 1922 the County Hall, which the short-sighted parsimony of the opposition had postponed, was opened by King George V and his Queen. How little its need had been foreseen by its critics was shown by the fact that another wing was subsequently added, and even so, accommodation was less than was needed.

When in 1928 his aldermanic term ended, Lidgett was not wholly sorry, for it coincided with the winding-up of the Progressive Party, a task he was glad to escape. Twenty-one years of outstanding service came to an end, but the doctor's interest in and love of London did not end with them.

It was said of Lidgett when he was upon the Council that he 'could evolve a formula for which everyone could vote quite happily, and not discover its ambiguity till later'. If this were indeed so, it was in no way due to deliberate smartness of the type which unscrupulous partisans sometimes exhibit. Lidgett was the soul of honour and quite incapable of the least trickery. Rather was it that he could be so persuasive and make out so good a case for what he was urging that others felt that it must be what they wanted. Later, perhaps, they saw it had implications which their minds were not sufficiently far-seeing to grasp at the time. But for that, they could hardly blame Lidgett.

Critics spoke of Lidgett's arguments as 'ponderous', and supporters called them 'weighty'. Both agreed, however, that logic, not rhetoric, was characteristic of them. He was of a serious type of temperament, and seldom called upon the humorous to aid him. He was unhurried and could not be 'rattled'. Tenacious and impressive he always was, whether in victory or defeat. He kept his temper and dignity in all circumstances. In all the many councils and committees, civic and religious, to which he belonged, he had the power to command respect. Those who did not agree had to listen and think. In debate Lidgett possessed a real flair for finding the right moment of intervention and saying the right thing at the right time. Nobody wished to have him on the other side when a motion they supported was under discussion. His leadership on the County Council had taught him how to bear with obstruction and defeat, to meet 'Triumph and Disaster' and 'treat those two impostors just the same'. He was conscious of the Divine Will in all things and saw in his secular duties a divine commission. It was this, more than anything else, which sustained him.

As a fitting close to this brief record of Lidgett's work for London, one may quote the letter written to him by Edwin Bayliss, D.L., J.P., then chairman of the LCC and dated 3rd November 1952.

'Dear Dr Scott Lidgett:

'I am so sorry that absence abroad prevented me from attending personally the ceremony on the 22nd of October last. On return here today, I should like one of my first actions to be to send you a message of most sincere congratulations on the honour conferred on you by Bermondsey Metropolitan Borough Council. Your admission to the honorary freedom of that borough comes as a distinction most truly deserved. I know that I speak for the whole Council here when I say that we are most grateful to learn of the high recognition which Bermondsey has so rightly accorded you, and which your long years of public service in that borough have so fully merited.

'In the name of the Council of which you were so long a valued and devoted member, I send you cordial greetings and good wishes. By their action in honouring you in this signal way, Bermondsey people have indeed spoken not only for themselves but for the whole people of London.'

LONDON UNIVERSITY

The public school and university doorway through which so many of our leaders pass into their careers was not for Scott Lidgett. He was well taught in a good private school at Blackheath, but the death of his father put an end to the hopes he had of going to Oxford or Cambridge. His school interests had been in classics, but these were laid aside to matriculate at London University, and then followed a couple of years in an office. Then his uncle and guardian, convinced that the youth's call to the Ministry was serious, allowed him to go for three and a half years to University College, London. Religious tests had but lately been abolished at the two older Universities and tests for fellowships there still existed. Lidgett's guardian was set against his nephew entering either of them, on the ground that the atmosphere and companionship would not help his Methodist convictions and determination to enter the Ministry. So in 1873 Dr Lidgett entered University College, which had been founded less than fifty years before. Its aim was to offer wider education on more liberal lines than had hitherto been possible, owing to the strong religious and clerical atmosphere of Oxford and Cambridge. It was regarded at first with much suspicion. Calverley lampooned the critics with barbed words:

> *It's a terrible crisis at Cam and at Isis:*
> *Fat butchers are learning dissection,*
> *And looking-glass makers become Sabbath-breakers*
> *To study the laws of reflection.*
> *Ye dons and ye doctors, ye provosts and proctors,*
> *Who are paid to monopolize knowledge,*
> *Come, make opposition, with voice and petition,*
> *'Gainst the radical infidel college.*

In those days London University was purely an examining body. Its foundation was later than that of University College, and though the students of that college took London degrees by examination, it was not until 1907, subsequent to London's becoming a teaching University, that the college was incorporated into it. How little could young Lidgett, studying philosophy at University College, have imagined himself Vice-Chancellor of London University! It was to philosophy and logic that Lidgett turned from classics, and in them found a discipline congenial to his mind. It was also in these subjects that he obtained his degree of M.A., at a time when it was said that the London M.A. was the hardest examination, taken entirely in writing, in the world.

Amongst Lidgett's teachers at University College were W. K. Clifford and Croom Robertson. Clifford's Agnosticism and Robertson's Associationist psychology were both ordained to be shredded later by the brilliant criticism of William James. Lidgett, the young keen student, was able, even before James's exposure of his teachers, to see the unattractiveness of their doctrines. But philosophy appealed to him, and he thought at one time of making it a special study together with theology. Had he done so, he might have made a noteworthy contribution to the philosophy of religion. But both studies were set aside when he heard the call that led to the founding of the Bermondsey Settlement. For many years Lidgett's connexion with London University was no more than that of being one of its graduates. But a much more intimate relationship was ahead. After the foundation of University College, under Whig and 'free-thinking' influences, King's College was founded in 1832 by the Duke of Wellington and others as a college on an Anglican basis, on a site in the Strand given by the Government. University College had for some time been attempting to gain powers to grant degrees. It was clear that if its request was granted, King's College would have to be given equal powers; two degree-giving bodies would be manifestly unsuitable—hence the University of London, which received its charter in 1836. The Government accepted the responsibility of housing the new University. At first it was in Somerset House, then for a couple of years in Marlborough House, and in 1855 in Burlington House, until a new building was erected in Burlington Gardens in 1870.

The University was purely an examining body, as we have seen. Pupils of King's and University colleges were permitted to take its degrees provided they had satisfactorily fulfilled their terms at college. The same applied to other approved institutions. It became evident that the certificates supplied by many of these were of very different values and the Senate had no powers of inspection of college and curriculum. Hence in 1858 the idea of being an examining body for students who had received college training was abandoned, and attendance at a college was not insisted upon, except for degrees in medicine. The University thus became an imperial university, and candidates from Britain and all parts of the empire presented themselves at London examinations. In 1867 the Senate was empowered by addition to its charter to hold examinations and grant certificates to 'female candidates', who were duly segregated for the purpose. This proved unsatisfactory, and by a further supplemental charter in 1878 the distinction was abolished, and men and women students were put on terms of absolute equality in all respects.

In 1900, after years of discussion and controversy, the University became a teaching, not merely an examining, body. It embraced all the principal colleges, in all subjects, within the greater London area, and in a few cases outside it. Following upon this, University and King's Colleges became incorporated in the University. The other colleges became schools of the University, including the medical schools and, in the faculty of theology, the Methodist College at Richmond. In 1926 a further Royal Commission made recommendations embodied in the University of London Act of that year, and new statutes were drawn up which came into force in 1929. One of the chief changes was the division of the work of administration, the Senate continuing the educational side, and a new body, the Court, the financial side—a division which worked well, despite the forebodings of many.

London University became the largest in the Empire and one of the largest in the world. The internal students, that is to say those taught in colleges and schools of the University, grew to be more numerous than those of Oxford and Cambridge together, whilst the examinations of the University were still open to external students, that is to say all outside the colleges and schools, who studied at other, non-degree-giving colleges, or independently.

London University, starting in this way, did not try to emulate the position of the older Universities, with their ancient colleges, distinguished past and long traditions. It had to find a new method of University life. Ever since the initiation in 1870 of universal schooling, and year by year with the growth of educational facilities in the country, it was clear that even for physical reasons the older Universities could never embrace all who were seeking a University education. Hence the development of the new Universities in London and the provinces.

Though without the advantages of the older Universities, London, by its very lack of traditions, could fulfil a function which they found it much more difficult to attempt. It could make experiments. From the very beginning it abolished all tests of religious belief. It was the first University to recognize that the English language was a necessary subject in education, as much as and even more than Latin and Greek. It gave a degree in English, having made it a compulsory subject at Matriculation. It was the first University to grant equality to women. It gave degrees in science, whilst the older Universities, though teaching science, still confined the name of the degree to arts. Its position in London made it the largest and most important of the Universities teaching medical science, with the most famous medical schools embraced within it. Most of these changes have been adopted by the older Universities, but London led the way.

One development of University policy pioneered by London University was University Extension work. Extension courses enable teachers to continue their studies after their college days are over. Not teachers only, however, because the courses are open to all, and it is surprising to see how many ordinary citizens, men and women alike, want to continue education in middle life. I have lectured at a number of such courses and examined for many more. Only this year I gave top place and seventy-nine per cent to a nun who had sat for an examination upon the philosophy of Thomas Aquinas, and whose age was the same as her marks. In one of my own courses, held during the months of the worst winter we have had since the War, one member, a lady, never missed a single lecture. I inquired from the secretary the age she had put down on her entrance form, and the reply was: 'I am afraid, like many of her sex, she is inclined to understatement in this respect. She entered herself as eighty, but I believe she is eighty-five.'

Extension work is not without its critics. A member of the Senate stated his opinion to that Body during the discussion of the report upon the Extension Department, that these courses gave only a shallow smattering of knowledge and that it was used pretentiously. This brought me to my feet to ask if any member of the Senate who chanced to get into conversation with his taxi driver would be surprised if the taximan asked his opinion of the theory that St Paul wrote four, not two letters to the Corinthians; for I had been reading the examination paper of a taximan who had taken an extension course on the New Testament and had written very well on that point. The Senate was obviously impressed. Except for the theological members, it is most unlikely that any of that august body had ever heard of such a view. Most of them probably imagined that a London taximan was a stout red-faced individual whose conversation would more likely than not be confined to an inquiry if his fare knew a good thing for the three o'clock! The critic sat silent.

No one was more pleased with this development than Lidgett. He had taken a central part in the institution of a diploma in biblical studies, and was energetic in promoting every type of Extension work. It was wholly in accord with his ideas of what a University should do to carry education outside its own circle to the people. Most of the leaders of London University were from the older Universities and whilst in one way this was an advantage, in another it was a handicap. Lidgett was free from the not unnatural bias of those whose training had been in what might be called the boarding-school universities, as contrasted with the day-school type which embraced external students. Whilst he was keenly interested in the development of the internal side of London University, he was always the champion of the external students, of whom he had himself been one. 'I believe in privileges', he declared, 'so long as they are privileges open to anyone who is worthy of them.' This indicated his attitude toward the student who wants to learn but is unable to enter a University.

It is not surprising that when London University expanded from being an examination board to a teaching institution, difficulties arose, especially among those who held its degrees with pride. The graduates whose diplomas had come from the London University of the past were convinced that the idea of teachers taking part in the examination of their own students was perilous in the extreme. They were certain that the high standards hitherto required would be lowered and the degrees they had obtained by much labour would be cheapened for ever.

Their fears were exaggerated but not groundless. The London B.D. examination, for instance, was a much more formidable affair when first it was instituted than it is today. What the objectors failed to see was that a University course, with its expert teachers and the association of one's fellow students, is more likely to prove educative than the mere passing of a difficult examination, often by correspondence tuition and intense 'cramming'.

However, it was External versus Internal in those days. Although Convocation has no great part in the direction of the University, it does elect a block of members to the Senate, and these of course were all on the External side. At first the examinations were kept apart, and even so the internal papers were subject to the scrutiny of an external examiner who had to certify that, in standard and marking, they were equal to those of the external side. Otherwise a student who, shall we say, took the Intermediate examination as an internal student and then left college would not have been allowed to sit as an external candidate for the final.

When Lidgett was elected by Convocation to the Senate, the first stage of animosity was over. It was then seen that soon there would need to be further changes in the constitution of the University, which took place eventually by the Act of

Parliament of 1929. Although representing the external side, Lidgett was statesman enough to see that the future lay with London as a teaching university, not as an examining body. He had no sympathy with the extremists who wished to close down the external side altogether, though he desired that everything should be done to encourage directed study and those university colleges which sent in their pupils for London degrees. Lidgett would never have agreed to bar the 'midnight-oiler' from his chance of a degree, and the private student can still obtain whatever London University has to offer in the way of degrees, excepting, of course, in the faculty of Medicine. Lidgett, himself an external student, had the chance of reconciling the two contending parties in no small degree, and one must give to him some share of credit for the present system, in which external and academic students, in most faculties, take a common examination. Whilst he was the friend of the external student, Lidgett's statesmanship was fully awake to the future of London University as the greatest teaching University in the British Commonwealth.

It has been necessary to give this outline of how London University came to be what it is, in order to indicate the importance of the connexion of Lidgett with it. At London he was able to take a position and exercise an influence which would have been almost impossible elsewhere. In 1922, he was pressed by friends to stand as a candidate for election to the Senate, among the members of that body whom the statutes permitted the graduates to elect. He doubted if there was any particular service he could do, for, as already said, he looked upon his work as part of his duty to use what powers he possessed for the wider service of the Kingdom of heaven, not simply for the Methodist or even the universal Church. He also wondered if he could find the time. Happily, his doubts were overcome, and he was duly elected as a representative of Convocation.

A majority of the members of the Court are elected by the Senate, and when the former body came into being, Lidgett was one of those elected to it. At the same time he was appointed Deputy Vice-Chancellor. This office, which is held for a year, is usually one without duties, for the Deputy is called upon to act only if the Vice-Chancellor is unable to fulfil his functions. As it befell, because of the illness of the Vice-Chancellor of 1929, Lidgett had to undertake much of his work; and he did it so well that the following year he succeeded to the office of Vice-Chancellor[1] and held it for the customary period of two years. I had been appointed to the Senate as a representative of the teachers of the University in Divinity in 1928, and had every opportunity of seeing and judging how the doctor fulfilled the task laid on him.

Much that was of unusual importance fell to his lot. The Chancellor, as at most Universities, is a person of distinction, but is not expected to undertake many duties in the exercise of the office. H.M. the Queen Mother is the present Chancellor. Lidgett had the unique experience of installing two Chancellors. Owing to the illness of the Vice-Chancellor, it fell to him to install Earl Beauchamp; on the latter's early resignation of the office, Lidgett now Vice-Chancellor himself, installed the Earl of Athlone. It fell to his lot to welcome the British Association to its centenary meetings in London in 1931, and to confer an honorary degree on General Smuts, its president that year. His speech on that occasion lacked nothing of those qualities which made him a master of assemblies.

Lidgett had 'the applause of listening senates to command', for he never lacked a hearing. The custom of the Senate was that on the expiration of ten minutes, the Vice-Chancellor should rise from his seat and don his cap. That signified that other speech should stop. The member speaking sat down and the Vice-Chancellor then said: 'The honourable member has been speaking for ten minutes. Does the Senate wish to hear him further?' I have known occasions when dead silence followed. The Senate was not so impolite as to return a more vocal negative, but in this case silence could speak. More often, however, there were cries of 'Go on', but sometimes these were few and feeble and the speaker wisely took the hint.

[1] The post of Deputy Vice-Chancellor is not necessarily a stepping-stone to the Vice-Chancellorship: it cannot be, as the Vice-Chancellor is usually elected for a second year, while the Deputy holds office for one year only.

It was an excellent rule to secure that although important speech could be extended, loquacity was made unwelcome, and most speakers planned what they had to say to occupy not more than the allotted span. Lidgett was not in general a particularly short speaker, but he seldom exceeded the ten minutes rule in the Senate, and if he did, he was almost certain to be encouraged to continue his innings till the next intervention at any rate. He spoke only when he had something to say, and he knew how to say it too.

He became a member of Convocation in 1875 and remained a member till his death seventy-eight years later, a record which must be almost without parallel. It was as a representative of the arts graduates that Convocation elected him to the Senate and he continued to represent them until he retired in 1946. He was reluctant to withdraw, but though 'his eye was not dim nor his natural force abated', he was then ninety-two and he felt it incumbent upon him to make way for a younger man. The University made note of the occasion by conferring upon him an honorary degree at the Foundation Day celebrations of that year. London University is somewhat sparing in bestowing honorary degrees, and only those of outstanding merit in their services to the community are offered the honour. Some expected that the doctorate of literature would be given, not Divinity, as the doctor already had been honoured by receiving this elsewhere. But the choice was Doctor of Laws. The wags said it was because Lidgett had great powers of laying down the law! It is customary for one only of those honoured by the conferment of a degree to speak afterwards, and to represent the rest. Lidgett was selected for this task and fulfilled it admirably in a speech short, incisive, and witty. There had already been the usual flow of oratory on such occasions. When the doctor sat down, the Member of Parliament for the University, the late Sir Ernest Graham Little, who was seated next to me, turned to whisper in my ear: 'The speech of the evening.' It was.

To preside over the Senate is an ordeal for any man. It consists of some fifty distinguished persons representing many sides of learning and ability. During my twenty-three years membership of the Senate, I held the office of Deputy for one year, and as the Vice-Chancellor happened to fall ill, had to take his place in the chair of the Senate. I am not a nervous subject, but I think I had a quicker heart-beat than usual that day! Dr Lidgett was commonly believed to have no nerves. He certainly showed none, but ruled the Senate with an easy mastery on every occasion.

I recollect the late Lord Dawson of Penn, the royal physician, once speaking against a motion. When the vote was put, Lord Dawson was whispering to his neighbour, and he absent-mindedly raised his hand when the Vice-Chancellor called for 'Those in favour'. This did not escape Lidgett's keen eye. 'Does the noble Lord wish us to judge him by his deeds or by his words?' he inquired. Lord Dawson hastily brought his hand down! Those who knew Lidgett more closely, however, knew that he could feel the stress of the greater occasions just as more ordinary people do. When he was Vice-Chancellor, the conferment of honorary degrees fell to his lot in the absence of the Chancellor. There were a number of highly distinguished men receiving degrees on that occasion, among them the Archbishop of Canterbury, Dr Lang. It was a curious sight for a Free Churchman, like myself, to see His Grace kneeling before Lidgett, as he was invested with the robes of his degree! When the ceremony was over, Lidgett called me and asked in noticeably anxious tones: 'Did I do all right?' I was able to assure him with conviction that in my opinion both his speech and his conduct of the ceremony were faultless, and he was obviously pleased.

The work of the Vice-Chancellor was not all of this sort. To the office there was attached membership of every important committee of the University, and so strenuous are its duties that some Vice-Chancellors have been given practically leave of absence from most of their duties elsewhere, to fulfil the demands made upon them by the high office they have assumed. Lidgett carried on his public and Methodist duties, taking the Vice-Chancellorship in his stride, yet doing as much in regard to it as any of his predecessors had done. One of the University staff, in amazement at the prodigious capacity for work the doctor showed, avowed to me: 'The man is not human; he is made of steel. No, not that. They say steel tires.' Some idea of Lidgett's commitments in this respect is given in the list of his services to the University at the end of this chapter. We must remember, too, that he was not one of those who belong to committees and never attend them. His only difficulty was that he never solved the problem of how to be in two places at once.

Creation, that is to say creative work, was his recreation. His holidays were found mostly in change of work. I recollect running across Dr Dinsdale Young[2] in the train, and, to my utter amazement, saw he was reading one of Edgar Wallace's books. 'I'm astonished, Doctor', I exclaimed. 'I thought I'd find you reading John Trapp, the prince of commentators, as I heard you once describe him.' Dr Young replied, with a twinkle in his eye: 'Ah, yes, but the bow must be unbent sometimes.' But when I saw Lidgett in the dining-car of the Atlantic Coast express, with the meal and all its distractions proceeding, lo and behold, he was reading a ponderous theological tome. 'I should find it difficult to read that at any time, most of all under these conditions', I said, not daring to remark that the doctor was enjoying a cigar also. 'Then', was the reply, 'you have not practised full mental control.' I sorrowfully agreed.

During Lidgett's term of office at the University, a number of important occasions befell. The University was housed at the Imperial Institute, South Kensington, a centre that was not 'central' and was too small. Long and fierce debate gathered around the inevitable extension. Some wanted to go to Holland Park, but wiser counsels prevailed, and the Bloomsbury site, adjoining the British Museum, was chosen. King George V laid the foundation stone in 1933 and since then the great buildings have continuously expanded and still expand.

The centenary of the University fell in 1936, and London was amazed at the brilliantly coloured procession of delegates from Universities all over the world, whose robes out-vied the

[2] Minister of the Central Hall, Westminster, for twenty-three years.

rainbow, as they went to St Paul's Cathedral for the service, which was followed by a luncheon at the Guildhall.

The appended list of Lidgett's University activities speaks for itself, but it does not mention the China Committee, because this was an inter-university affair. It arose out of the Government's decision to give part of the Boxer indemnity as a fund to create deeper cultural relations between China and Britain. Of this Committee Lidgett was a member, and, after his term was fulfilled, was unexpectedly recalled. The chairman, the Master of Balliol, resigned, and the committee were of one mind that the man to take his place in the chair was Lidgett— a fact which speaks for the regard he had won for himself not only in London, but in the other Universities of the country.

His interest in Westminster College, the Methodist training-college for men teachers, was, as others in this book have pointed out, in part due to the fact that his grandfather, the Rev. John Scott, had been its Principal, and as a boy he had played in its grounds. He said that this was one reason that he valued the chair of the University Training Colleges Delegacy to which the Senate appointed him. He was also a governor of Queen Mary College, which, being in the East End, appealed to him because of his deep knowledge of the poorer quarters of London. He was equally interested in his governorship of Royal Holloway College, at Egham, the 'Girton' or 'Newnham' of London University.

When, during the War, London University took over my own college at Richmond, one of its divinity schools, for its administrative staff, and the college was badly damaged by a flying bomb, it was to Lidgett that I turned, with expectancy that was not disappointed, for help in getting the essential repairs permitted, so that the college could carry on. From first to last his motto might well have been the royal '*Ich Dien*' —'I serve'. His service to London University left results which will never be lost, and those of us who were both teachers of the University and Methodists will always be proud of him, and thankful to God for what he was and did in our University.

DR LIDGETT'S RECORD WITH THE UNIVERSITY OF LONDON

    1871 Matriculation Examination
              Placed in First Division
              Entered from Blackheath Proprietary School
    1873 First B.A. Examination
              Placed in First Division
              Student at University College
    1874 Second B.A. Examination
              Placed in First Division
              Student at University College
    1875 M.A. Examination—Branch III
              Placed fourth in list of six
              Student at University College
    1875 Became a member of Convocation

  1922–46 Member of the Senate as one of the representatives of the registered graduates in Arts
  1929–30 Deputy Vice-Chancellor
  1930–32 Vice-Chancellor
    1946 Received honorary degree of Doctor of Laws at Foundation Day celebrations (28th November)

Committees of the Senate

  1922–46 Council for External Students
  1928–29 Academic Council
  1924–29 Board to Promote the Extension of University Teaching (in 1929 this became the University Extension and Tutorial Classes Council)
  1929–32 }
  1933–45 } University Extension and Tutorial Classes Council
  1934–39 Matriculation and School Examinations Council

  1923–26 Ad eundem Degrees Committee
  1926–27 Committee on the Report of the Departmental Committee on the University
  1927–29 Site and Buildings Committee

1930–33	Committee on the Medical Education of Women Undergraduates
1933–39	Boat-House Committee
1929–32 1933–46	Committees Revision Committee
1930–47	Committee of Management of Connaught Hall (Dr Scott Lidgett was Chairman of the Committee of Management for the whole of this period)
1930–44	Committee of Management of the Courtauld Institute of Art
1930–46	Finance and General Purposes Committee
1930–46	Honorary Degrees Committee
1928–46	Training Colleges Delegacy
1940–46	Emergency Statutes Committee
1929–43	Member of the Court. Dr Scott Lidgett was one of the original Senate members when the Court was formed in 1929

He served on the following Committees of the Court:

1929–30	Grants Committee
1930–31	Allocation of Grants Committee (above Committee renamed)
1930–31	Estate Management Committee

ERIC S. WATERHOUSE

THE ECUMENICAL STATESMAN

CHAPTER SIX

THE ECUMENICAL STATESMAN

IT is abundantly clear, from several chapters in this book, that Scott Lidgett's primary and overriding interest was theology, that his whole career in all its manifold and variegated aspects was a full-scale attempt to express, in terms of Church loyalty, social service, universal education, and public service, the theology of the Fatherhood of God as revealed in the Incarnation of Jesus Christ. Other men have seen, and acted upon their vision, that the Gospel needs to be applied to this or that part of human life; Scott Lidgett saw, and acted upon his vision, that the Gospel in its very nature as the Gospel embraces the whole of human life and can only be expounded fully if the whole range of human activities and interests is included in the exposition. Other men have supported their interest in the welfare of humanity and their compassion for human suffering by asserting in a general way that the love of God for man impels them toward philanthropy; Scott Lidgett worked out precisely, from the study of the New Testament and of historical theology, what is meant by the love of God, and how it is integrally connected with the active love of man for man.

It will occasion no one any surprise, therefore, to learn that Lidgett's persistent activities for the reunion of Christendom were theologically based, and that his theology of reunion, and of the nature of the Church in general, was an essential part of his general theological system. It is most fully expounded in *Apostolic Ministry*, published in 1909, and in *God, Christ, and the Church*, published in 1927, and dedicated to Randall Davidson, Archbishop of Canterbury (each of these two works being a collection of essays, articles, and addresses, on various related themes); these two books go very easily together, for it does not seem that Lidgett changed his view on any central issue during the intervening years. But it comes out again and again in his writings and utterances on all sorts of occasions, chiefly, perhaps, when he was addressing such bodies as the Wesleyan Methodist or the Methodist Conference, or one of the Councils of the Free Churches.

What, then, is the basic conception of Lidgett's 'theology of reunion'? Without question, a biblical doctrine of the Church, its nature, its ministry, and its catholicity. He begins a discussion of reunion in *God, Christ, and the Church* by relating the Kingdom of Christ to the Church of Christ. The Kingdom of Christ, or the Kingdom of God, with which he identifies it, was widely interpreted throughout the first thirty years of this century in Great Britain as something very much of this world, either as the new order of human society, without war, poverty, or suffering, for which men of goodwill were striving in every country, or more vaguely, as the right ordering of spiritual energies in such a way as to produce happiness, peace, and plenty, for all mankind. But after the first World War a very different interpretation of the Kingdom was brought to the notice of British theologians by Continental scholars, whose experience of wartime and post-war Europe chimed in with new approaches to the teaching of the Gospels to repudiate all Utopian conceptions of the Kingdom as humanistic and stupidly optimistic, and to produce the doctrine that the Kingdom does not belong to this world at all; it is transcendent, cataclysmic, apocalyptic, coming down upon man from God and by the sole gift of God in the Parousia of Jesus Christ. On the first two, optimistic and evolutionary, conceptions of the Kingdom, it is the business of the Christian to be up and doing, to build God's Kingdom, or at any rate to advance and extend it; on the third view, pessimistic of all man's powers and relying solely on God's intervention in human affairs, the Christian is to stand waiting for his Lord's appearing, to continue, indeed, with his prayers and with his daily work, but not to suppose that his poor efforts will affect in any way the date or the character of God's Kingdom.

Characteristically, Lidgett is not prepared to support any of these views of the Kingdom without reserve; he offers, rather, to 'combine the elements of truth they severally represent in a more comprehensive whole'. The theologians of today might say that he gives too much credit to the Utopian view, by taking the parables of growth and life in the Gospels to indicate that the Kingdom comes partly by the development of human powers. This may be true, but it is also true that he gives proper emphasis to the pre-eminent place of God in His own Kingdom, and shows that all its blessings come by the grace of God alone. He seeks, in other words, to hold together the this-worldly and the other-worldly conceptions of the Kingdom in one whole, thus, as he claims, understanding it dynamically rather than statically. But his decisive word on the Kingdom of God comes when he reminds us that the King for the coming of whose Kingdom we are to pray in the Lord's Prayer is first of all addressed as 'Our Father'. The Kingdom of God is a family, in which God wills that many sons should be brought to glory by the redemption offered to all mankind by His only-begotten Son, Jesus Christ our Lord. Thus he can conclude: 'Only the Kingdom of Christ can make progress living, effective, and permanent by bringing to it, throughout its entire range, the strength and succour of the Divine Fatherhood conveyed through the realization of Sonship.'

Having thus brought the Kingdom of God and the Fatherhood of God into so close a relationship, Lidgett proceeds to consider the relation of the Church to the Kingdom. He refuses to allow that the Church is truly defined as the instrument by which the Kingdom is advanced and through which it comes, though he acknowledges that the attempted definition suggests an important truth. Nor, of course, will he agree to the identification of the Church with the Kingdom—the identification which since St Augustine has distorted men's understanding of the Gospels and sent the Roman Church down so many false paths—though he ascribes more value to it than Protestants have usually been willing to grant. He turns to the Epistle to the Ephesians—the Epistle from which he never wanders very far when he thinks of the purpose of God for mankind—for the words which will suggest the true definition. He declares that the 'mystery' which the Apostle is charged to 'make all men see' is that 'the Gentiles are fellow-heirs and fellow-members of the Body, and fellow-partakers of the promise in Christ Jesus through the Gospel'. The missionary calling and success of the Church show that in it a gift of life and salvation is enjoyed of which all men are by their very nature capable; everyone can be a partaker of the blessings of God's Kingdom. The Church consists of those who have actually become partakers of them. So it is 'a kind of first-fruits'; it is, in fact, 'the earnest and anticipation of redeemed mankind, which is to be gathered together into Christ's Kingdom by being brought to the enjoyment of those Divine relations of light and life and love into which believers have already entered by virtue of their restored and fulfilled Sonship'. The Church is already what God purposes that all mankind should become, and it is set in the world to bear witness to all men of what God has in store for all men, and here and now wishes all men to receive. It is 'a living embodiment of the grace which it conveys'. It is the community of those who belong to the Kingdom of God, formed with the express purpose that those who do not yet belong to it may be brought into it, and that meanwhile those who do belong to it may receive in personal and social life the good gifts of God that accrue to those who are the sons and subjects of their Father-King.

It follows at once from the nature of the Church, that the Church is one and only one; for the purpose of God for mankind is that it should grow into perfect unity, into the measure of the stature of the fullness of Christ, into the one hope of our calling; and the Church is the foretaste, the antepast (as Charles Wesley might have called it) of that perfection. Moreover, it is part of the Church's function to witness to the unity of God. Therefore, on all grounds, the unity of the Church must be asserted, and Lidgett asserts it in no uncertain tones. The Church, he says, is not a human creation but a divine gift; and part of that divine gift is its unity. 'The Church manifests the unity of the Father and promotes the unity of mankind by means of a ministry of reconciliation, which as the activity of the one Spirit gives practical effect to our Lord's *atoning* work. . . . Mankind is destined through the ministry of the Church to be brought into unity of life with the one God and Father through the one Christ, and, as the consequence, into the unity of a common consummation which transcends, if it does not abolish, all human distinctions whatsoever.' For the fulfilment of its own destiny, and of the destiny of mankind through it, God has made the Church to be one Church; 'unity is the immanent ideal of the Churches' life'.[1]

By its divided state the Church contradicts the law and purpose of its being and renders itself unfit to fulfil its high destiny. That it has become divided constitutes the great tragedy of its history. Lidgett has a very clear conception and account of the way in which divisions have taken place. Episcopacy, that is the rule of the local Church by a single president, arose naturally and properly after the New Testament period to cement the fellowship of Christians; each local Church in due course had its own bishop, and the bishops became the 'recognized organ of intercommunication throughout the Church to its remotest bounds', and thus the bond of unity between all Christians; the holding of local, provincial, and ecumenical Councils provided further means by which the universal fellowship was established and confirmed. But unfortunately the Church began in course of time to take over the institutions of Imperial Rome, and with the institutions it took over their power and pretensions; when the Roman Emperor vacated his place in Rome, the Bishop of Rome filled the vacancy, and 'in exercising spiritual authority substituted Imperial government for fellowship as a means of maintaining Christian unity throughout the world'. Thus the Church, meant by God to be one in faith and hope and love, was forced into an unspiritual unity by institutionalism, centralization, and power-politics; 'faith, the ordinances of worship, and spiritual influence, were converted into law, governed by regulation and enforced by dread ecclesiastical sanctions'. This hardening of the Church's arteries, this substitution of power for love, led, inevitably, first to the conflict between East and West which resulted finally in complete schism, and

[1] *God, Christ, and the Church*, pp. 219-30.

then, a few centuries later, to the Reformation and the total break-up of the unity of Christendom.

Lidgett thus puts the blame for Christian disunity chiefly at the door of the Roman Church, and disposes effectively of the Roman claim that the rest of Christendom has wilfully and wrongfully separated itself from Rome, the true and only Mother of the faithful. But this does not mean that he regards the Protestant Churches as 'innocent and void of offence'. On the contrary, he charges them with imitating Rome by imposing upon themselves 'an undue emphasis on the distinctive types of ecclesiastical organization', so that they also in turn erected barriers against universal fellowship and urged their own claims to the exclusion of those of others; thus the dreadful entail of schism and separation was continued, and plagues the Church to this day, almost to its complete destruction.[2]

The Church, then, is one in its essential nature; but it is grievously divided. In our day, says Lidgett, God is calling it to express in its outer life the unity which belongs to it, to be seen of men to be what it is in the eyes of God. He does not plead for uniformity of worship, organization, and beliefs—very far from it—but he argues unmistakably for the outward reunion of the Church, as the only possible way of embodying and proclaiming to the world its inner, God-given unity. He takes issue very vigorously with those who suggest that we do not need outward unity, but only spiritual, invisible unity. His chief ground of complaint against them is that they are 'simply reflecting and justifying the existing state of things'—they are making a virtue of their disinclination for change and their unwillingness to take the risk of losing institutions which they value. The very fact of Christian fellowship 'is a living force which constrains (those who enjoy it) to seek bodily form and expression for it, in order that it may be completed, safeguarded, educated, and made known. The vitality of the spiritual fellowship and its veracity, to say the least, vary directly with the desire to give corporate manifestation and enforcement to it, as is the case with every other form of human fellowship and agreement.' Man, in other words, is not

[2] op. cit., pp. 265-8.

a purely spiritual being; if he possesses a spiritual reality, he is bound to give bodily expression to it in the form of an institution or a sacrament, for otherwise it will fade away and die. 'All denominations—Roman, Eastern, Anglican, as well as Nonconformist—speak provincial dialects, which betray their lack of fulfilled catholicity. . . . Such catholicity as belongs to each denomination, be it more or less, can only be preserved in so far as it energizes in the active pursuit of more.'

He is equally severe against those who oppose outward reunion on the ground that, in history, divisions sprang out of regard for truth, and have therefore helped rather than hindered the advance of Christ's Kingdom. He agrees that divisions have often happened because elements of truth have not been fully recognized, or have become obscured by those who professed to preserve them. But the divisions have, he contends, done as much harm as good to the truth in the long run, and the best that can be said of them is that they have acted in the advancement of truth much as wars operate sometimes to the overthrow of evil things; we acknowledge wars to be evil, and so also we should acknowledge divisions to be evil. For, however much gain to truth these divisions may have sought to achieve, 'the sinfulness, imperfection, and limitations which made these divisions inevitable, set their mark for evil upon the apprehension of the very truths in behalf of which they were caused'.

He deals very fully and carefully with those who wish the divisions of the Church to continue in order that freedom may be preserved, giving full weight to their contention that the 'tendency of all societies, however progressive may have been their original aims, is to become stereotyped'. He admits that this has happened many times to the Church, and that the effect of it has been to destroy 'liberty of prophesyings', to check growth and dry up the springs of life. What has happened in the past, he confesses, might happen again in the future, if the Churches are brought once again into organic unity. Lidgett has here a difficult case to answer, because in so many respects he is on the side of those who work for progress in the face of ecclesiastical restrictions; he was not without personal experience of the petrifying effect of tradition, and he hated a dull uniformity and a heavy-handed authority. His knowledge of Church history, as we have seen, gave him ample grounds for supposing that a unified Church is often a hardened, inflexible Church, incapable of further development.

But he disposes of the 'argument from freedom' by a double attack. Firstly, he claims that faith is not a purely personal thing, though of course it is personal; the very fact that it is personal makes it also social, for by being personal it is self-communicative; it lives by sharing, it dies by keeping itself to itself. Thus faith by its very nature requires a community in which it is to be expressed, and that community must include all those who share their faith with one another. Faith, it is true, requires and demands freedom, but it also contains within itself the drive toward unity. In the one, ideal, Church the progressive, personal elements of faith are truly and properly balanced with the elements which are conservative and social. The second line of attack is the demonstration that the very forces of freedom, the dynamic by which the Church is now advancing to new developments, tend in our time toward unity and not division. It is true, says Lidgett, that from time to time the potent forces within the Church pull in opposite directions, upsetting the equilibrium which is the true embodiment of the Church's nature. This happened at the Reformation, it may happen again in the future. But in the present a new stability is asserting itself, and the inward logic of the Church's own being is demanding outward recognition. The Church is called upon by the guiding Spirit to make the venture of faith for the sake of unity.

Having first stated the theological argument for unity, and defended it by considerations of Christian history and the Christian understanding of man's nature, Lidgett is prepared to offer some pragmatic considerations by way of supplement. It would have been contrary to his whole outlook to start from expediency; but he is prepared to bring in expediency when the rights of theology have been established. So he argues, in language which needs only slight changes to be identical with what has been uttered from many pulpits (and ought to have been uttered from more) since the second World War, that the state of the world and the Church makes reunion imperative. The League of Nations is seeking to prevent the causes of war, he says, and in this endeavour deserves the support and welcome of the Churches. But how can the Churches bear sincere and conscientious witness to the brotherhood of mankind when they are themselves divided? 'How can the Church denounce the pride, the self-sufficiency, and the discordant ambitions that stand between the nations and the final order of peace, when exactly these same vices, in a subtler form, are a fatal obstacle to its own unity?'

Again, how can the evangelization of mankind be successfully taken in hand by a divided Church? 'Why should the peoples of India, China and Africa be expected either now or eventually to face and fight their way through the tangled history of Western Christendom?' Again, the moral standards of mankind are being endangered by changing social and international conditions. How can the Church give the necessary guidance and help in a changing world, how can it bring its whole force to bear upon any point that is threatened, except by means of complete and organized unity? Finally (here Lidgett speaks in full and anxious awareness of the post-war problems of his country—he is writing in the early twenties), the task of social reconstruction is laid heavily on the nation. The Church will surely wish to play its full part in gaining for every man and woman their rightful share in the benefits which God has showered on mankind. But the witness and work of the Church in these matters are seriously hampered at every turn by its divisions; 'our "unhappy divisions" prevent us from having one mind, speaking with one voice, and manifesting the glory of a self-sacrifice that has attained its full vigour by triumphing over the most insidious forms of faction and self-seeking'.[3]

Lidgett's teaching about the nature and unity of the Church is at all points undergirded by his conception of Catholicity, which an earlier chapter has shown to be integral to his whole theological position.[4] Catholicity, he says, is sometimes

[3] op. cit., pp. 230-40.   [4] See p. 105, *supra*.

misunderstood as acquiescence in dogmatic truths, and sometimes as the exercise of and submission to divinely delegated authority, dispensed by priests. But it is something quite different: it is the fellowship of a great spiritual experience, conveying the truth in a living, self-confirming revelation, and the marks of such an experience are the great biblical affirmations—adoption as sons, redemption through Christ's blood, the forgiveness of our trespasses, hope in Christ, the sense of quickening and of heavenly exaltation, reconciliation, access through Christ and in one Spirit to the Father, the knowledge of the love of Christ, fellowship with the saints through common access to God. The Catholic Christian is the man who has shared in all these things; the Catholic Church is the Church that is the witness to all these things, and from it no Catholic Christian is excluded. It should be observed that Lidgett never for a moment excludes the Roman Church, in spite of its sins and errors, from the Catholic Church. He says indeed that Catholicism has been the worst foe of Catholicity, but he adds that denominationalism, if exaggerated, may be equally fatal.

The Catholic Church has its own distinctive ministry, and that ministry is, for Lidgett, definitely described in the Epistle to the Ephesians. The scope of such a ministry is never narrower than mankind; it seeks all nations ('taking the whole world as its parish'), and the last and lowliest of the human race. It offers the 'unsearchable riches of Christ' on the strength of a deep, ever-growing experience of those riches. It is a ministry of illumination, assuming and appealing to a divine capacity everywhere present (here we have a recurrent idea of Lidgett's, vulgarly known as belief in 'a divine spark in every man', now somewhat discredited in theological circles). It builds up the Church as a fellowship of believers and the first fruits of mankind, an earnest of the blessed reunion of all mankind in the citizenship of the saints. It helps in the accomplishment of God's final purpose for mankind by building up His Church in this way. It involves the joyful acceptance of hardship and difficulty, and a positive sharing in the sufferings of Christ and mankind; it is fulfilled and perfected only by ceaseless prayer and intercession. This means that the distinctive type of catholic ministry is not the doctor or the ruler, as in Catholicism, but the preacher. 'Under that comprehensive calling are included the special yet kindred offices of apostles, prophets, evangelists, pastors, and teachers.' Here, of course, Lidgett discloses his Methodist upbringing and convictions, and perhaps also throws a sidelight on his conception of his own variegated ministry.[5]

It is worth noticing that Lidgett does not find it in any sense necessary to vindicate the right of the ministry of his own Church to a place in the Catholic ministry of the whole Church of God. That right was to him obvious and indisputable. But in an important passage in his Presidential Address to the Wesleyan Methodist Conference of 1908, he shows the catholicity of Methodism and indicates the part which it is called to play in the restoration of the full Catholicity of the Church, temporarily lost by its divisions. Methodism, he says, inherits the full historic tradition of Catholic Christianity. 'Who, save ourselves, can separate us from it? ... As we look out upon history and upon the world, it is with the same vision of all things in Christ which dominates the perception of all believers, without distinction of age, or race, or Church.' At the same time it has to be affirmed of Methodism that it came into existence by the work of the living Word and the quickening Spirit of God; and its coming into existence in the eighteenth century meant little less than the re-creation of Christianity in England and the re-establishment of civilization.

From this, Lidgett goes on to discourse at large upon the place of the various Communions of Christendom in the history and the coming unity of the whole. All the great forms of Christian life are interdependent; each embodies distinctive aspects of Catholic truth. In some ages it has been necessary to accentuate differences in order to restore neglected truths. But the truths that were then contended for can later be reconciled in the larger synthesis of a reasonable faith which holds together the separate contentions which kept the ancient combatants apart. The present age can be an age of such

[5] The argument of the last two pages comes from the Ordination Charge delivered to Wesleyan Methodist ordinands in 1909 (*Apostolic Ministry*, pp. 106-29).

reconciliation (it is worth remembering that Lidgett said this before the great Edinburgh Conference of 1910, which is usually given as the start of the Ecumenical Movement). The beliefs, ideals and duties of our common Christianity should be far more powerful to unite us than our differences to estrange or divide us; in fact, our minor differences can help us into intimacy and co-operation. Only thus can the vast tasks of the twentieth century be fulfilled.

Then Lidgett proceeds to his magisterial outline of the ecumenical tasks of the Wesleyan Methodist Church: 'Where there are no differences, our watchword must be union; where they are comparatively slight, federation; where they are more serious, yet not destructive of the fundamental agreement of Christianity, co-operation in order to defend and promote the supreme interests and applications of our common Christian life.' And he addresses to his fellow-leaders in the Methodist Church the word that ought still to strike home: 'The schismatic is always a traitor.'

What Lidgett applied directly to the Wesleyan Methodist Church he of course applied in general to all the British Free Churches, and would have applied to all the Churches of Christendom. To British Free Churchmen, meeting in the National Free Church Council in Birmingham in 1906 under his Presidency, he announced that their Council was a concrete expression of the ideal of catholicity, not just a meeting of like-minded enthusiasts who wished to discuss their common problems; it embodied the prayer of Christian people that they might all be one. It showed also that Free Churchmen were not content with a mystical, secret unity, but sought outward, visible expression of their spiritual unity in Christ. Yet the source and inspiration of such a unity did not lie in any theory of the Church, for the very nature of the Council was incompatible with the beliefs that any particular form of ecclesiastical organization was exclusively divine. The bond of unity was 'in common faith in Christ, in discipleship to His mind, and in loyalty to His authority'.

But it is clear from what has already been said that Lidgett could never be content with a Catholicity that included the

Free Churches only, however great were the difficulties in bringing into being a larger unity. He therefore went on to say that the effort at unity could not be confined to the Free Churches, and that he longed for the time when all the causes of separation should have passed away. The apparently negative affirmations of the Free Churches needed to be made in the interests of true Catholicity, for they indicated that Free Churchmen refused to identify Christianity with any one form of ecclesiastical institution or to magnify any office in the Church, even the office of the Ministry, beyond its proper importance. But, in fact, the Churches in the Free Church Council represented Protestantism on its positive and constructive side, standing for freedom alike in Church and State, for the infinite responsibility of the individual, for his direct and unmediated access to God in Christ. Yet they had no monopoly, nor the completeness, of Catholic truth, and Protestantism itself had still to reveal the full glory of its spiritual meaning and comprehensiveness.[6]

The most striking thing about Lidgett's ecumenical theology is that it is fully up to date. If we strip it of the phrases which suggest the immanentism which was characteristic of the first part of the century, and of those which suggest a more optimistic view of human progress than subsequent events have borne out or biblical thought warrants, and come down to its real content, we shall find that Lidgett was already saying before the first World War and just after it the things which the best ecumenical theology of today is now saying, and often believes itself to be saying for the first time. The Church as the foretaste of the glory that is to be revealed, that is (in the modern jargon), as an eschatological reality, the Church's God-given unity and the consequent imperative to be outwardly what it essentially is, the Catholicity of the Church as containing and transcending all its differences—all these are familiar conceptions to those who take part in the modern ecumenical conversation. Lidgett was a pioneer in expounding them. But he expounded them before the Churches were willing to hear them, and he expounded them in oracular, resounding periods

[6] *Apostolic Ministry*, pp. 229-34.

which tend rather to deaden than to enlighten the modern mind. If his words had been heeded by those who heard them and read them, it is possible that the movement toward Christian unity would have gone farther than it has, and would have been brought home to a greater number of ordinary Church members.

Having thought out the theological basis of reunion, Lidgett moved, as always, inexorably into action. He began in the sphere of personal relationships. He was not a man to whom intimate personal friendship came easily, nor one whose personality was a great incentive to it in others. Nor did he have the advantage in this matter that has come to many of his younger successors, the advantage of University friendships within the Student Christian Movement—mostly, but not wholly, at Oxford and Cambridge—cutting right across the denominations (the leaders of the Ecumenical Movement today are in many cases the leaders of the Student Christian Movement and the World Student Federation of twenty years ago grown up). Even if Lidgett had been an undergraduate at Oxford or Cambridge, it is very doubtful if he would have had in those days the free exchange of ideas and close spiritual fellowship with those of other traditions which are possible and common, and vastly beneficial, today. Yet in spite of these handicaps, Lidgett realized the value of personally knowing those with whom he might later be discussing difficult matters of doctrine and Church Order, and the lessening of theological misunderstanding and denominational suspicion which results therefrom.

A notable example of this is provided by Lidgett's relations with Edward Stuart Talbot, Bishop of Rochester and later of Southwark and Winchester. Talbot in the early years of his episcopate was a fairly stiff Anglo-Catholic. In his later years he became more flexible, and was very anxious for the fullest kind of co-operation that was consistent with his principles. He came to regard the Church of England as partly responsible for the various separations from her which had taken place, and though he continued to refer to the Free Churches as 'bodies', he wrote to one of his clergy: 'The language which talks of all Dissenters as schismatic is abhorrent to me, because

I feel that the ills of schism—which are very great—are historically and otherwise the common guilt of us all.'[7] It is perhaps not entirely fanciful to suggest that the development of his views on the relations between the Anglican Church and Free Churchmen was in part due to the personal contact with Lidgett which began when Talbot became Bishop of Rochester in 1895 and came to live in Kennington. Lidgett and Dr F. B. Meyer, the noted Baptist minister, collaborated to arrange for a party of Free Church ministers to call on the new Bishop and welcome him to the district. From that time the friendship between Lidgett and Talbot grew, and Lidgett invited the Bishop to the opening of the first picture exhibition at the Bermondsey Settlement. Talbot declined the invitation, fearful that his presence at the exhibition would be misunderstood. But a few years later he sent to Lidgett a volume of his recently published sermons, and Lidgett reciprocated the gesture with *The Fatherhood of God*. The Bishop's reading of this book during an illness helped to persuade him that Free Churchmen were not heretics after all, and he subsequently commended it to the clergy of his diocese for the continuance of their theological education. Lidgett and he remained in close personal touch, and often met in ecumenical discussions. Just before leaving Southwark for Winchester, Talbot came to the Bermondsey Settlement to open a picture exhibition in the same series as the one which he had refused to grace at the beginning of his episcopate, and in 1932 he sent a letter of warm congratulation to Lidgett on his becoming the first President of the Methodist Church re-united.

Even more significant was Lidgett's friendship with Randall Davidson, who was Talbot's predecessor as Bishop of Rochester before being translated to Winchester on his way to Canterbury. About this Dr G. K. A. Bell, Bishop of Chichester, Davidson's biographer, shall speak:[8]

'Dr Scott Lidgett and Archbishop Randall Davidson knew one another for nearly thirty years. Their first contact was in 1891,

---

[7] *Edward Stuart Talbot*, by Gwendolen Stephenson, p. 115.
[8] In a note specially written for this volume.

when Davidson was appointed Bishop of Rochester and made his home in Kennington. Their personal acquaintance began somewhat later; it ripened through co-operation in many causes, and during and after the first World War grew into a close friendship, the significance of which was signalized by Scott Lidgett's place as a pall-bearer at the first part of the Archbishop's funeral service in Westminster Abbey in 1930. There can be no doubt of the admiration which Davidson felt for his ability and statesmanship, or of the trust which he reposed in him as a great and representative Christian leader. Indeed, throughout his primacy there was no Free Churchman to whom Davidson turned with greater confidence for advice and counsel, knowing Scott Lidgett to be not only thoroughly alive to the great public questions of the day and sensitive to moral issues, but also a very sound judge of reactions in Free Church circles. There was a robust common sense in the character of each which made for mutual liking and confidence.

There were two fields in particular in which relations between Davidson and Scott Lidgett were markedly close and in which they saw a great deal of one another—religious education and Christian unity. The Fisher Education Act of 1918 led to a variety of conferences between Anglicans and Free Churchmen on the subject of religion in schools and the various problems connected with the dual system. Indeed such conferences had already started before 1918, the ground being to begin with by no means easy. In all of these Scott Lidgett took a leading part. He was of course thoroughly alive to the traditional Free Church point of view. At the same time he was equally alive to the great desirability of a national system being achieved which would secure adequate provision in all public elementary schools for religious observance and instruction, differentiated so far as practicable in relation to religious tenets, subject to a conscience clause. Scott Lidgett was never wanting in resolute advocacy; but he was also very much a practical man, concerned to get the best possible result in given circumstances. The two men approached the schools question certainly from different angles, but they were both moderate and constructive. No settlement was in fact achieved. But the spirit by which each was guided had its own powerful influence on the whole educational atmosphere. It was very different from the heated days when Birrell, Runciman, and McKenna were Presidents of the Board of Education in succession.

Scott Lidgett also took a particularly keen interest in the field of Christian unity. The *Appeal to All Christian People* issued by the Lambeth Conference in 1920 was a land-mark on the road to reunion. Scott Lidgett was a member of the joint committee set up by the Free Church Federal Council in September 1920 to examine the *Appeal*, to prepare a statement, and to discuss certain proposals with representatives of the Anglican Communion. From 1922 to 1925 he was one of the most regular and active Free Church members of the joint committee of Bishops and Free Church leaders which met constantly at Lambeth, and of its inner committee of thirteen, of which I was secretary. It was he who, with Dr. Carnegie Simpson, welcomed with profound appreciation the crucial statement of Archbishop Lang, recognizing non-episcopal ministries of the Free Churches represented on the conference as "ministries of Christ's Word and Sacraments within the Universal Church of Christ which is His Body".

The conferences ceased in 1925. Archbishop Davidson died in 1930. They were resumed after the Lambeth Conference of 1930 and continued till 1938. And all through, Scott Lidgett played a conspicuous part. But he had a prominent share in every department of the general movement for Christian fellowship. He was, as far as I can trace, the first British churchman in this century to formulate and publish a clear plan for a council of Churches, small in numbers, to consist of the principal leaders of the Churches of Great Britain (apart from the Church of Rome) with the Archbishop of Canterbury as ex-officio chairman. He was one of the founder members of the British Council of Churches inaugurated in 1942, and though a very old man he continued to the end to give his steadfast, and, when there was need, vocal support to all for which it stood.

It is also a matter of interest to know that he took the same line as Archbishop Davidson with regard to the policy of reprisals in the first World War, and in his appeals to the nation on the occasions of the Railway Strike in 1912 and of the General Strike in 1926, besides being favourable to the Enabling Act of 1919, which gave certain powers of self-government to the National Assembly of the Church of England.

Scott Lidgett was an admirable speaker in his prime, swift to see the point, and vigorous in the expression of his views and in the development of his argument. Further, being a man of just mind and ready to understand the opinions and convictions of others, he was a master of conciliation. Last of all, he was not only wise and shrewd, and one who gave continuous and devoted service to the nation as a great Free Church statesman, but he was also a very kind-hearted human being.'

The field of ecumenical activity into which Lidgett threw himself first of all was that of Free Church Unity. In spite of what they had in common, the Free Churches (more usually known as the Nonconformists, or even as the Dissenters, until the end of the nineteenth century) had not done very much together until Dr Guinness Rogers, a leading Congregationalist minister, contributed to the *Methodist Times*, at the request of Hugh Price Hughes, the editor, an article recommending the holding of a Free Church Congress. This was in February 1890. The suggestion was at once supported by Free Churchmen of several denominations, and the matter was freely canvassed. In 1892 (and again in 1893 and 1894) Dr (later Sir) Henry S. Lunn invited the leaders of all the Churches in England, including the entire bench of bishops, together with Mr Gladstone, to a conference on Christian unity in the pleasant surroundings of Grindelwald, in Switzerland. A sufficiently large number of those invited (not including Mr Gladstone) took advantage of this handsome offer to make the conversations very well worth while, but it became clear as they proceeded that the time had not yet come for definite proposals to be made about co-operation between Anglicans and Free Churchmen. The Free Churchmen present, however, were able to develop the notion of Free Church co-operation into practical plans, and, not least as a result of their Alpine deliberations, a Congress of Free Churchmen was held in Manchester in November 1892. This was an assembly of invited persons, and it was soon followed by the setting up of Free Church Councils in many parts of the country, and by further Congresses in Leeds (1893) and Birmingham (1895). The first Congress had no difficulty in deciding that the Free Churches were in substantial agreement on the doctrine of the Church, the Ministry, and the Sacraments, as well as on the other evangelical doctrines. Dr Charles Berry, the Congregationalist, and Hugh Price Hughes were tireless in their advocacy of the cause of Free Church co-operation, and it was above all due to their nation-wide efforts that Free Church Councils sprang up in so many places, and that in 1896, at Nottingham, the National Council of the Evangelical Free Churches was formally constituted.

There was, naturally, a strong body of opinion which wished the Council to be officially representative of the denominations, but Hugh Price Hughes fought vigorously, and in the end successfully, against this. He held that if the Council became too official it would be prevented from holding the free discussion which he believed to be the breath of its life. It was settled that the membership of the Council should be territorially based, and that the representatives of the local Free Church Councils, themselves based on the individual congregations, should constitute it. Whether this was the right constitution or not, there is no doubt that the Council at once began to fulfil a very valuable function. It published a Free Church Catechism, which demonstrated both the orthodoxy and the unity of the Free Churches beyond argument. It conducted many evangelistic missions up and down the country, and one on a national scale in 1901. In 1908 it was claimed on its behalf (but this claim cannot really be verified) that the Council spoke for 'roughly half the religious community of the country', and it had become what Hugh Price Hughes had dreamed for it in 1894, 'a Nonconformist Parliament for our common objects, composed of those who believe in the divinity of our Lord, Jesus Christ'.

In 1916 it seemed to several leading members of the Council, and most of all to J. H. Shakespeare, the Secretary of the Baptist Union, that the time had come to transform the Council, by regular stages, into a United Free Church of England. Shakespeare had propounded the idea some years before, and now, as President of the Council, he persuaded the Council to initiate positive discussions with a view to drawing up a scheme of union. Each of the denominations appointed a delegation to meet in conference in 1916 and 1917, and in 1917 a plan for a Federal Council of the Free Churches, formed by their official representatives, and intended by many of its sponsors to be a step toward organic union, was produced. It was greeted with enthusiasm by the Baptists, the Congregationalists, the Presbyterians, and the smaller denominations, but with a certain lack of fervour by the Wesleyan Methodists. The Federal Council came into existence in 1919, and the Wesleyan Methodist Conference sent representatives to it after a year or two of its existence. But it never went very far in the direction of a United Free Church. Nor was it in the true sense of the word 'Federal', since the denominations which were represented on it were in no way committed by any of its decisions, though they were morally bound to consider them carefully. The Federal Council was, however, the body with which the representatives of the Church of England held the conversations which resulted from the Lambeth *Appeal* on Christian Unity in 1920.

Thus there were two Free Church Councils in existence during the period between the two World Wars. The personnel of their leading supporters and members was often very much the same, and some of the functions of the two Councils overlapped; a 'Nexus Committee' sought to harmonize their activities. But the fusion of the two Councils was inevitable, and took place in 1940; the Free Church Federal Council was born on 16th September of that year during an air raid at the height of the Battle of Britain.

There is no doubt that at its beginnings the National Free Church Council was the expression of a militant Nonconformity, eager to dislodge the National Church from its privileged position and to battle against Canterbury and Rome on every issue where the rights of free Englishmen in general, and Free Churchmen in particular, seemed to be endangered. Such militancy was perhaps then necessary, as was shown by the education controversies of the first years of this century. But it is pleasant to record that it has steadily given place—more slowly, of course, in some localities than in others—to a desire for co-operation and mutual understanding between Free Churchmen and Anglicans, and the Diamond Jubilee Congress of the Federal Free Church Council in 1956 was marked by an appeal by its Moderator, the Rev. K. L. Parry, for a united Church in England of all the denominations (except the Roman, which excludes itself).

Throughout most of the nineteenth century the Wesleyan Methodist Church had occupied a somewhat ambiguous position between the Church of England and the 'Dissenters', sympathizing with both but not belonging to either. But as the century drew toward its close the weakness of the Evangelical party within the Church of England and the growing strength of the Anglo-Catholics, and not least of their Ritualistic section, steadily alienated the sympathies of Methodists from the Established Church and drew them into the Free Church camp. The dominating personality of Hugh Price Hughes completed the process, and so it was that Wesleyan Methodism played a leading role in the formation of the National Free Church Council.

Scott Lidgett took a minor part in the negotiations which led up to this; and when Hugh Price Hughes died, his mantle fell on Lidgett in Free Church matters, as in so many others. He was President of the National Council in 1906, and Honorary Secretary from 1914 to 1940, and from then on Honorary Secretary of the Federal Free Church Council. He was Moderator of the Federal Council of the Evangelical Free Churches from 1923 to 1925. He took an active part in the important Committees of all three Councils, and was constantly called into counsel on matters of policy, of doctrine, of public affairs, and of education in particular.

He was never, however, in sympathy with militant

Nonconformity. He looked upon Free Church unity as a stage on the way to the complete unity of English Christendom, never as an end in itself. In 1912 and afterwards he gave his support to J. H. Shakespeare's notion of a united Free Church, again as a step toward the greater united Church of the future. He seems, however, to have come to regard Shakespeare's scheme as impracticable, and he was probably much happier to work for a Federal Council than he would have been with a plan for a united Free Church. He represented the Federal Council in the unofficial discussions with Anglicans which preceded the Lambeth *Appeal* of 1920, and again in the official conversations which took place afterwards.

Of all the signs of growing understanding between the Church, and of the 'coming great Church' which were visible in his life-time, none seemed more hopeful and fruitful to Lidgett than the Lambeth *Appeal to All Christian People*. Archbishop Davidson had deliberately put the matter of reunion on the agenda of the first Lambeth Conference after the 1914-18 War, against the advice of Bishop Gore, who suspected that 'reunionists yielded themselves to their amiable instincts and did no clear thinking', and that their zeal would lead the Anglo-Catholics to break away from the Church of England. The reunion committee of the Conference contained many doughty Anglo-Catholics, as well as those of more moderate temper, and for a long time it could not agree on a proposal to bring before the whole Conference. Then it was suggested that not a series of resolutions, but an appeal to all Christian people, would meet the case best of all. The *Appeal* was drawn up and carried the unanimous support, first of the Committee, then of the whole Conference, which signified its approval by the spontaneous singing of the doxology.

The *Appeal* called on all Christians to face the terrible facts of a broken Christendom, to see the vision of Christ's one Church and then to go forward to make it come true. It acknowledged the share of the Church of England in the guilt of division, and laid it down that reunion could be achieved only on the basis of the so-called Lambeth Quadrilateral, wholeheartedly accepted—that is, the Scriptures, the historic Creeds of the undivided Church, the Sacraments of Baptism and Holy Communion, and 'a ministry acknowledged by every part of the Church as possessing not only the inward call of the Spirit, but also the commission of Christ and the authority of the whole Body'; it added that in the judgement of the assembled bishops the historic episcopate was the one means of providing the necessary ministry. An essential part of the *Appeal* was the express refusal to call into question the 'spiritual reality of non-episcopal ministries', which 'have been manifestly blessed and owned of the Holy Spirit as effective means of grace'.

Lidgett was enthusiastic in his eagerness to follow up the *Appeal* with practical negotiations—even to the length of approving the initiation of the Malines Conversations between unofficial spokesmen of Rome and Canterbury. He was very active in the discussions between Anglican representatives and the representatives of the Federal Council. He was firm in his support of the Free Church subordination of Order to Faith, in the affirmation of the spiritual principles of the Reformation, in the vindication of Free Church ministries as true and valid ministries of the Word and Sacraments. But he never allowed the goal of reunion to fade from his mind—or from the minds of his co-representatives—and always sought to be conciliatory and firm at the same time. He willingly adhered to the Free Churchmen's acknowledgement that the united Church of the future would be episcopal in government.

The discussions were suspended in 1925, that there might be a pause for reflection, and the question of the status of Free Church ministries was left unsolved; there was no agreement as to whether the ministries at the act of union between the Church of England and the Free Churches should be united by mutual commissioning or conditional ordination, or in some other way yet to be worked out. The Lambeth Conference of 1930 was not so eager for the promotion of reunion as had been its predecessor in 1920, and the discussions between Anglicans and Free Churchmen which followed it (and in which Lidgett, of course, took a prominent part) did not make much progress. Yet Lidgett, writing in 1936, was not discouraged, and he deplored the impatience of some in these words:

'Before Reunion is accomplished, all the Communions concerned must be convinced that *God wills it*, and must make a concerted demand for its achievement. This result, however, is, as yet, far from having been attained. The existing and still prevalent denominationalism is, in all the Churches, an amalgam of particular loyalties, habits, and prejudices. In a good many Free Church meetings I have, for example, been called upon to join with the congregation in singing Faber's well-known hymn, "Faith of our Fathers living still". Obviously, for Faber this faith was that of the Roman Catholic Church. But for the older Nonconformist Churches it is, above all, the Faith as it was held by the Reformers and Puritans, while for Methodists it means the inheritance they have received from John and Charles Wesley. With equal intensity all these sections join in singing the same hymn, but both the emphasis and content are, in each case, different, and, in important respects, divergent. Hence the problem is not merely intellectual and practical. It is, above all, psychological. Until the enthusiasm evoked by the hymn becomes concentrated upon the same content of belief, transcending the existing, but narrower, loyalties, habits, and prejudices, the result of all this fervour may well be to fortify differences rather than to promote that inward Catholicity which is the precondition of Reunion. The friends of Reunion must, therefore, devote themselves to the prime necessity of overcoming differences and estrangements by bringing about the Unity of Faith, so that a common emphasis shall subordinate these differences, and all our "prophesying" may be "according to the proportion of the faith".'[9]

Enough has been said to indicate the theological principles which underlay, and the practical wisdom which directed, Lidgett's zeal for the reunion of Christendom. We need not doubt that he would have strongly approved the arrangement of Conversations, with a view to intercommunion, between representatives of the Church of England and the Methodist Church, to begin in 1956, and would have prayed fervently for their successful outcome. In tune with this are certainly his

[9] *My Guided Life*, pp. 249f.

words at the Ecumenical Conference at Oxford in 1951. After paying grateful tribute to John R. Mott, present at Oxford, as the author of the great Edinburgh Conference of 1910, and after showing how the Churches, as a result of that Conference, had learned the value and fullness of their common unity in their confession, 'Jesus is Lord', he continued: 'Wherever that confession is truly made, there is the communion of saints. This includes the Roman Catholic Church, despite our serious differences from it. We thank God that that Church has handed down to us the Creeds, the writings of the Fathers, and has given us numerous examples of holy and effective leadership in the pursuit of truth and righteousness, of faith, hope, and love in Christ Jesus our Lord. All those who confess "Jesus is Lord" belong to one another, and their catholicity is mightier than the differences which at present divide them. So Methodism, in fulfilling John and Charles Wesley, must go forth in the utmost endeavour to promote the fellowship, the unity, the eventual union of all who "profess and call themselves Christians" throughout the world.'[10]

RUPERT E. DAVIES

[10] *Proceedings of the Eighth Ecumenical Methodist Conference*, p. 237.

INDEX OF NAMES

ADDAMS, MISS JANE, 51
Arnold, Matthew, ix, 41, 113, 132
Anselm, Archbishop, 88, 92, 94
Athanasius, Archbishop, 92
Athlone, Earl of, 175

BARNARDO, DR, 56
Barnett, S. A., 47, 49ff, 55, 62f, 76, 138
Barnett, Mrs S. A., 47, 50, 62
Barth, Karl, 102, 104
Bayliss, Edwin, 167
Beauchamp, Earl, 175
Beet, Dr J. A., 68
Benn, Sir John, 164
Bell, Bishop G. K. A., 199
Berry, Dr Charles, 203
Birrell, Augustine, 140, 164, 201
Booth, Charles, 54, 72, 74
Borland, John, 60
Bowden, George, 11
Brunyate, W. E., 59
Bucer, Martin, 98
Bunting, Jabez, 9f
Bunting, Sir Percy, 65
Bushnell, Dr F. J., 89
Butler, Bishop J., 42
Butler, Josephine, 138
Butler, R. A., 145, 150f

CAMPBELL, J. MCLEOD, 84, 89
Campbell-Bannerman, Sir Henry, 139f
Clarke, Dr Adam, 10
Clifford, Dr John, 134, 140, 149
Clifford, W. K., 169
Coley, Samuel, 11f
Collier, S. F., 56
Cowper-Temple, Mr, 126

DALE, DR R. W., 68, 83, 88f, 94
Dallinger, Dr W. H., 21f
Dante, 95f
Davidson, Archbishop R., 4, 147, 151, 187, 199ff
Davies, Dr Andrews, 17
Dawson of Penn, Lord, 177
Denison, Edward, 48f
Denton, George, 21
Dixon, Joseph, 164

EDE, J. CHUTER, 152
Erskine of Linlathen, 84

FABER, F. W., 208
Fairbairn, Dr A. M., 83, 134
Fawcett, Millicent, 138
Fisher, Archbishop Geoffrey, 5
FitzGerald, W. D., 117
Forster, W. E., 126

GARVIE, DR A. E., 66
Gater, Sir George, 144
Gell, Lyttelton, 50

George V, 166, 178
George, David Lloyd, 132, 140
George, Henry, 61
Gladstone, W. E., 70, 203
Gooch, G. P., 65
Gore, Bishop Charles, 5, 58, 78, 138, 206
Gorst, Sir John, 127f
Green, John R., 40, 48
Green, T. H., 91, 138
Grotius, Hugo, 88, 94

HALLOWELL, J. HIRST, 141
Hare, J. C., 86
Harrison, Dr A. W., 127, 149f
Henderson, Arthur, 69
Holland, H. Scott, 138
Hopkins, Miss Ellice, 17
Hopkins, Sir R. V. N., 59
Hort, Bishop F. J. A., 83, 104
Howard, Dr Wilbert F., 103
Hughes, Hugh Price, 20f, 26, 56, 64f, 86, 96f, 117, 128, 133, 138, 202f, 205

JAMES, WILLIAM, 169
Jeffery, Dr G. B., 146
Jones, Dr J. D., 66
Jones, Dr J. V., 116
Jowett, Dr B., 50, 86

KEEBLE, S. E., 64
Kelly, C. H., 117
Ker, Dr W. P., 116
Kidd, Benjamin, 47
Kimmins, Dr C. W., 59
King, Bolton, 50
Kingsley, Charles, 83, 86

LAMBERT, BROOK, 48
Lang, Archbishop C. G., 151f, 177, 201
Lansdowne, Lord, 25
Lassalle, Ferdinand, 47
Lewis, Major Norman, 61
Lidgett, George, 13
Lidgett, John Jacob, ix, 9f
Lidgett, Mrs J. J., ix, 10
Lidgett, Mrs J. Scott, 17f, 57, 63
Lightfoot, Bishop J. B., 83, 104
Little, Sir E. Graham, 176
Lofthouse, Dr William F., 60n
Lowndes, G. A. N., 134
Lunn, Sir Henry, 202

MANNING, CARDINAL, 138
Marx, Karl, 47
Maurice, F. Denison, 47, 83ff, 89, 91, 94, 100, 102ff, 128f, 138
McKenna, Dr R., 141, 164, 201
Meyer, Dr F. B., 199
Mill, J. S., 47
Moberley, W. H., 94
Moody, D. L., 17
Morant, Sir Robert, 128, 131, 133

Morton, Miss Honor, 60
Mott, John R., 209
Moulton, Dr William F., 14, 22, 45f, 86, 117, 124f
Murray, Dr G., 40

NAIRNE, DR J. Alexander, 99
Newman, Cardinal, 64, 83, 95, 102
Noble, Dr Walter J., 153
Nunn, Hancock, 50

OSBORNE, DR, 86
Oecolampadius, 98

PARRY, K. L., 205
Passfield, Lord (Sidney Webb), 132
Paterson, Alexander, 72
Paton, Dr J. B., 18, 138
Peake, Dr A. S., 29
Perks, Sir Robert, 26
Pope, Dr W. B., 14, 16, 22, 45, 84, 114, 120
Priestley, J. B., 77
Pringle-Pattison, Dr A. S., 116
Pusey, Dr E. B., 64

RAMSBOTTOM, MR, 148
Randles, Dr Marshall, 22, 86f
Reding, J. Edwin, 32ff
Rigg, Dr J. H., 86, 128, 130, 133
Rippon, Mr, 61
Ritschl, Albrecht, 89f
Roberts, Dr T. R., 116
Robertson, Croom, 169
Rogers, Dr Guinness, 202
Rowntree, Seebohm, 72, 74
Runciman, Lord, 141, 201

SADLER, SIR MICHAEL, 139
Salter, Dr Alfred, 59
Salter, Mrs A., 59
Sankey, Lord, 151

Scott, John, ix, 9ff, 15, 112, 118f, 121f, 126, 131, 143, 179
Scott, Mrs J., 10
Shaftesbury, Lord, 83
Shakespeare, J. H., 204, 206
Shaw, G. B., 124
Simpson, Dr P. Carnegie, 66, 201
Simpson, Miss Ruth, 153f
Smith, Professor Lester, 126, 142
Smith, Sir Llewellyn, 74
Smuts, General, 175
Spiers, William, 164f
Stead, W. T., 138
Stephenson, T. B., 56
Strauss, David F., 91
Stuart, Professor James, 138

TALBOT, BISHOP EDMUND S., 5, 138, 198f
Temple, Archbishop, 66, 102, 149f, 152
Thompson, Peter, 56
Toynbee, Arnold, 50
Trevelyan, G. M., 40

VAUGHAN, CHARLES J., 17, 116

WATKINSON, DR W. L., 22
Watson, Richard, 88
Watts, Isaac, 101
Waugh, Benjamin, 138
Wellington, Duke of, 169
Wesley, Charles, ix, 6, 36, 65, 84, 101, 103
Wesley, John, ix, 6, 7, 9, 25, 29, 36, 65, 67, 84, 101, 103, 105, 208f
Westcott, Bishop B. F., 83, 89, 104
Whitehead, A. N., 100
Wilberforce, William, 83
Wiseman, Dr F. Luke, 34
Wolverhampton, Viscount, 14
Wood, McKinnon, 164

YOUNG, DR DINSDALE T., 117, 178

www.ingramcontent.com/pod-product-compliance
Lightning Source LLC
Chambersburg PA
CBHW070314230426
43663CB00011B/2125